**RETURN TO NORMALCY
OR A NEW BEGINNING**

RETURN TO NORMALCY OR A NEW BEGINNING

Concepts and Expectations for a Postwar Europe around 1945

Edited by

JOACHIM LUND

&

PER ØHRGAARD

University Press of Southern Denmark
Copenhagen Business School Press

Return to Normalcy or a New Beginning
Concepts and Expectations for a Postwar Europe around 1945

© Copenhagen Business School Press & University Press of Southern Denmark
Printed in Denmark by Narayana Press
Cover design by BUSTO | Graphic Design
1. edition 2008

ISBN 978-87-630-0203-5

Distribution:

Denmark
University Press of Southern Denmark
55 Campusvej
DK-5230 Odense M
Denmark
Tel + 45 66 15 79 99
Fax + 45 66 15 81 26
www.universitypress.dk

Rest of Scandinavia
DBK, Mimersvej 4
DK-4600 Køge, Denmark
Tel +45 3269 7788
Fax +45 3269 7789

North America
International Specialized Book Services
920 NE 58th Ave., Suite 300
Portland, OR 97213, USA
Tel +1 800 944 6190
Fax +1 503 280 8832
Email: orders@isbs.com

Rest of the World
Marston Book Services, P.O. Box 269
Abingdon, Oxfordshire, OX14 4YN, UK
Tel +44 (0) 1235 465500
Fax +44 (0) 1235 465655
Email Direct Customers: direct.order@marston.co.uk
Email Booksellers: trade.order@marston.co.uk

All rights reserved. No part of this publication may be reproduced or used in any form or by any means - graphic, electronic or mechanical including photocopying, recording, taping or information storage or retrieval systems - without permission in writing from Copenhagen Business School Press at www.cbspress.dk

Table of Contents

Preface
PICKING UP THE PIECES OF EUROPE IN 1945 7
Joachim Lund & Per Øhrgaard

Chapter 1
EUROPA 1945 UND HEUTE 9
Egon Bahr

Chapter 2
'OLD IDEAS IN NEW BODIES' 21
The Economic Reconstruction of Europe in 1945
Patricia Clavin

Chapter 3
'WITH EUROPE, BUT NOT OF IT' 33
British Thoughts on Future Anglo-European Relations
at the End of the Second World War
Jørgen Sevaldsen

Chapter 4
IN AND OUT OF EUROPE 51
Spain 1945
Carsten Humlebæk

Chapter 5
ALL ROADS LEAD TO ROME 63
Fascism and Anti-Fascism in Postwar Italy
Morten Heiberg

Chapter 6
FRANCE'S ROLE IN THE WORLD IN 1945 77
Back to the Future?
Bent Boel

Table of Contents

Chapter 7
NORDIC DESTINY OR EUROPEAN SOLIDARITY 93
Scandinavia at a Crossroads after the Second World War
Joachim Lund

Chapter 8
GERMAN WRITERS' ATTITUDE TOWARDS EUROPE
IN THE FIRST POSTWAR YEARS... 113
Per Øhrgaard

Chapter 9
EUROPE AS A VISIONARY IDEA 129
The European Discourse in West Germany
in the Decade after the Second World War
Axel Schildt

Contributors.. 141

Preface

PICKING UP THE PIECES OF EUROPE IN 1945

Joachim Lund & Per Øhrgaard

Europe, spring 1945. On May 8, the Allies received the unconditional surrender of the German Armed Forces in Berlin. In 2005 we celebrated the 60th anniversary of the defeat of Nazism and the end of the Second World War in Europe. But VE-Day not only signified the triumph and possible reestablishment of the prewar balance of power. It was also Day One of a postwar European development in which none of the key questions regarding Europe's future were settled – except perhaps issues relating to (most) national borders and the extent of US and Soviet spheres of influence and power. The winning side represented a variety of different and conflicting political views and economic interests, the fight between democracy and dictatorship had only just begun, and economic and logistic problems of supplying the populations of Europe continued to set the agenda.

In this situation, what were the expectations for Europe's future? What were the hopes and anxieties of the Western European populations? What were the ideas and plans of politicians, intellectuals and social engineers concerning the future of Europe? The Marshall Plan and the North Atlantic and Rome treaties lay far ahead, and plans of a closer relationship between the European states at best came in the shape of visions. Some preferred quickly to revert to business as usual, some favoured the idea of a new beginning and large-scale political and economic transformations. In many ways, Europe found itself at a crossroads.

In his famous speech to the *Bundestag* on 8 May 1985, *Bundespräsident* Richard von Weizsäcker commemorated the peace 40 years earlier: "Der 8. Mai ist ein tiefer historischer Einschnitt, nicht nur in der deutschen, sondern auch in der europäischen Gechichte. Der europäische Bürgerkrieg war an sein Ende gelangt, die alte europäische Welt zu Bruch gegangen (…) Es gab keine "Stunde Null", aber wir hatten die Chance zu einem Neubeginn."

A "new beginning" had already been on the agenda around the end of the First World War, but it was a controversial theme: in the USA the Democratic president Woodrow Wilson (1913-1921) and his idealistic attempt at creating a new world order was replaced by Republican Warren G. Harding (1921-1923), who won the 1920 election, promising the American voters to set a course back to the good old days, or to "normalcy", as he mistakenly put it. On the European stage, in 1945 as well as in 1918, many Europeans asked themselves if the continent would relapse into national isolationism or develop new ways of transnational co-operation.

The book addresses this fundamental postwar question. It is based on the conference *1945 – Back to Normal or a New Beginning? Expectations and Concepts for at Postwar Europe*, which took place at the Copenhagen Business School in September 2005. The various contributions dealt with the problems, dilemmas and expectations in the Western European scenario, as experienced by governments, organizations, groups and individuals working at the time of the *Kriegsende*. The aim was to pin down essential concepts and discussions about Europe's future, not only addressing issues that would eventually lead to the establishment of the European Union, but also embracing those that might have taken Europe in a different direction.

A revised version of the conference contributions is collected in this volume. A witness of history and a central figure in the German 'Ostpolitik' of the late 1960s and the 1970s, Egon Bahr looks back at the year 1945 and points out the differences between the Berlin and the West German perspective. Patricia Clavin explains the continuity of economic planning of the League of Nations from the inter-war period to wartime and postwar commissions and organizations. Jørgen Sevaldsen, Carsten Humlebæk, Morten Heiberg, Bent Boel, and Joachim Lund outline the situation in Great Britain, Spain, Italy, France, and Scandinavia in 1945, stressing the ambiguity of the impact of the war on politics and on the economy. Finally, the defeated Germany is the subject of the contributions by Axel Schildt and Per Øhrgaard.

We would like to thank Birgit Hüttmann, who assisted in organizing the conference, and Stig W. Jørgensen for technical assistance.

Copenhagen, autumn 2007

Joachim Lund   Per Øhrgaard

CHAPTER 1

EUROPA 1945 UND HEUTE

Egon Bahr

Meine Damen und Herren,

Jemand, der 1945 den Einmarsch der Roten Armee in Berlin erlebt hat, hat einen ganz anderen Bezug als den normalen der Westdeutschen zum Thema Europa.

Ich kann nur sagen, der Einmarsch der Roten Armee war nicht besonders angenehm. Aber das Wort Europa kam nicht vor, auch in meine Erinnerung nicht, unter dem Gesichtspunkt, dass man irgendwas, irgendwann in jenem Sommer an Europa gedacht hat. Oder sich auch nur den Begriff überlegt hat.

Meine erste, wenn Sie so wollen, *politische* Reflexion begann in dem Augenblick, in dem ich im August 1945 das Potsdamer Abkommen las. Und zwar deshalb, weil ich beim Lesen den Eindruck hatte: „Ach, das war's schon? Mehr nicht?" Also, das war völlig klar, Deutschland sollte keine Soldaten haben, natürlich nicht. Keine Waffen produzieren, natürlich nicht. Da waren noch ein paar Geschichten mit den Gebieten östlich von Oder und Neiße. Da kamen die Polen rein, die Deutschen wurden ‚herausgegangen'. Dass konnte man erwarten, dass es ein bisschen territoriale Verluste geben würde. Aber das Wichtigste war, wir sollten als Einheit verwaltet werden. Und wir sollten die Möglichkeit bekommen, durch eigene Arbeit uns wieder aufzurappeln.

Im Vergleich zum Versailler Vertrag – den wir übrigens in der Form in der Schule durchgenommen hatten, dass wir im Französischunterricht *Les consequences politiques de la Paix* von Jacques Bainville gelesen hatten; und dabei auch gelernt hatten, dass dieser Versailler Vertrag zu hart war um zu versöhnen, aber nicht hart genug, um das Gelüst nach Revanche zu unterdrücken – im Vergleich also zu Versailles war das Potsdamer Abkommen milde. Man hatte aus Versailles gelernt. Wir waren also dankbar.

Egon Bahr

Im Grunde: Mir ist erst später eingefallen, oder aufgefallen, dass das Kriegsende natürlich mit den Deutschen etwas gemacht hatte, was es vorher gar nicht gegeben hatte. Nämlich, uns war politisch das Kreuz gebrochen worden. Wir hatten, wie man im Deutschen zu sagen pflegt, die Nase voll. Von Macht, Waffen, Einfluss, Bedeutung, Gewicht. Wir wollten von dem ganzen Quatsch nichts mehr wissen. Insofern war die *re-education*, die dann begann, komisch und überflüssig. Wir wären auch ohne *re-education*, durch den totalen Zusammenbruch, durch die totale Niederlage, durch die Trümmer, durch die Toten, satt gewesen und wollten gar nichts mehr, was mit Macht zu tun hatte. Übrigens, niemand hat damals daran gedacht, dass die Deutschen mal wieder bewaffnet werden könnten, das lag völlig fern. Selbst 1949, als also die Bundesrepublik ein Grundgesetz bekam, haben die Alliierten, die das ja väterlich begleitet haben, um es milde zu sagen, großen Wert darauf gelegt, dass im Grundgesetz deutsche Soldaten nicht vorkamen.

Und erst etwas später als, im Verfolg von Korea, es notwendig war, dass man die Deutschen bewaffnete, weil die konventionelle Verteidigung der NATO nicht glaubwürdig gewesen wäre ohne die Deutschen, gegenüber der konventionellen Überlegenheit der Sowjetunion und des späteren Warschauer Paktes, – erst da haben wie das Grundgesetz ergänzt durch einen Artikel, der die Aufstellung einer Deutschen Armee betrifft.

Die Alliierten haben damals gesagt: „Aber wir wollen noch ein bisschen mehr. Doppelt genäht hält besser. Wir wollen, dass ihr in das Grundgesetz hinein schreibt: ‚Ihr werdet euch unter keinen Umständen an einem Angriffskrieg beteiligen.'" Das haben wir gemacht. Wir hatten ja keine Absicht, überhaupt Krieg, geschweige denn einen Angriffskrieg zu führen. Und niemand konnte sich 1954 vorstellen, dass ausgerechnet unsere mächtigsten Beschützer, die Amerikaner, mal einen Angriffskrieg führen würden. Und uns vielleicht dann noch fragen würden, ob wir uns daran beteiligen könnten. Also, wir sind friedlicher geworden als es viele später wollten. Oder als es vielen später gefiel.

Aber wie gesagt, jemand der in Berlin die ganze Entwicklung erlebt hat, jedenfalls bis 1949, als ich als Korrespondent nach Bonn kam, war von vornherein klar: Wir mussten mehr an die Amerikaner und an die Russen denken, als an die Engländer und die Franzosen. Europa lag uns fern, auch unter dem Gesichtspunkt der Ideale, der Visionen, der Vorstellungen. Vielmehr waren wir gezwungen, uns nach den Kategorien der Macht zu orientieren. Auch der militärischen Macht natürlich. Und unter diesem Gesichtspunkt war völlig klar: Wir konnten nur überleben dank der Garantie der Amerikaner, sonst wäre Berlin (West)

Europa 1945 und Heute

nicht frei geblieben; und wir mussten bedenken, welche Druckmöglichkeiten die Sowjetunion hatte. Und es war völlig klar, dass wir von Berlin her Europa ganz anders gesehen haben als von Westdeutschland her.

Es gab in Berlin eine Zeitung, die es heute noch gibt, den *Tagesspiegel*. Der wollte eine Zeitung für Deutschland machen, von Berlin aus, und er musste diese Absicht einstellen deshalb, weil sich herausstellte, dass diese Zeitung, von Berlin her, in Westdeutschland nicht zu verkaufen war. Weil schon damals klar war, dass man in Westdeutschland im Grunde westlich dachte; man guckte nur nach dem Westen, man wendete dem Osten den Rücken zu. Und die Überschriften waren eben jeden Tag anders in den westdeutschen und in den Berliner Zeitungen. Das heißt: Eine Spaltung des Denkens lief parallel mit der Spaltung der Stadt, oder der Spaltung des Landes. Noch anders gesagt, wir konnten Europa überhaupt nicht denken ohne Ost-West-Bezug. Wir konnten Europa überhaupt nicht denken, ohne Amerika und Russland – oder die Sowjetunion – im Blick zu behalten. Das heißt: Wir haben Europa im Grunde nie allein unter dem Gesichtspunkt Westeuropa gedacht. Das ist etwas anderes als das, was normalerweise in Westdeutschland und in Bonn gedacht wurde.

Die erste wirkliche Begegnung mit Europa gewann ich durch die Teilnahme an den Abschlussverhandlungen über den Schumanplan in Paris. Das war eine ungewöhnlich interessante Sache. Es war vor allen Dingen auch psychologisch Öl auf eine verwundete Seele, denn nun saß man wirklich mit einer der Siegermächte am Tisch. Na, Siegermächte haben wir damals auch schon mit einem Anführungsstrich versehen und haben gesagt, also die Franzosen sind Sieger *honoris causa*. Aber es war der Beginn, dass die Bundesrepublik wieder in die Familie der Völker einrücken konnte, akzeptiert wurde und dazu noch in einer Weise, die eine Perspektive eröffnete, die für uns viel größer war als die für Frankreich.

Von Frankreich her gesehen ging es um die Einbeziehung der Deutschen, der westdeutschen wirtschaftlichen Potenz in den Aufbau Westeuropas, damit auch um eine Kontrolle. Und für uns war die Perspektive: ‚Wir wollen wirklich nach Europa', also wir wollten die Schrecklichkeiten der nationalen Vergangenheit in Europa loswerden. Wir konnten hoffen, dass wir diese Lasten im europäischen Hafen parken könnten. ‚Europa' war deshalb von Herzen kommend, auf dem Hintergrund der totalen Niederlage. Wir waren die einzigen, die bereit waren, Kompetenzen, Souveränitäten auf Europa zu übertragen, und zwar *in*

Egon Bahr

toto. Wenn die Deutschen etwas machen, machen sie es gründlich. Also am liebsten wäre uns die Vollintegration Europas gewesen. Wir waren begeistert, als die Studenten die Schlagbäume zwischen Deutschland und Frankreich zerbrachen oder beseitigten. Und wir hatten festzustellen: Wir waren mit diesem Wunsch nach einer vollständigen Integration in Richtung der Vereinigten Staaten von Europa allein. Denn niemand wollte das. Weder die Franzosen, noch die Belgier, noch die Italiener, noch die Niederländer, auch nicht die Luxemburger. Das heißt, es war ein Zeichen dafür, dass die Deutschen ihre nationale Identität verloren hatten. Während alle anderen Staaten selbstverständlich ihre nationale Identität behalten hatten.

Das war auch die Zeit, in der ich Jean Monnet kennen lernte, einen bewundernswerten, genialen Mann, der ohne jede staatliche Macht, ohne jede staatliche Regierungsfunktion im Stande gewesen ist, die Politiker der sechs EG-Staaten, und dann auch einige darüber hinaus, zu überzeugen, egal von welcher Partei sie kamen, für eine Vision, Europa. Eine Vision Europa, die er im Prinzip schon in Amerika entwickelt hatte und die nun damals, als er sie entwickelt hatte, mit amerikanischen Freunden zusammen, natürlich darauf hinaus ging, dass diese europäische Zusammenarbeit – ‚Schumanplan' und was daraus wurde – die wirtschaftliche Flankendeckung für die NATO sein sollte. Die NATO hatte die Aufgabe, eine wirksame, abschreckende Verteidigung zu sichern, und die Überlegung war: Die Menschen sind nur bereit sich zu verteidigen, wenn es ihnen wirtschaftlich nicht schlecht geht, sondern möglichst besser geht. Die Zusammenarbeit: Wirtschaft, Schumanplan, EG war also gewissermaßen die wirtschaftliche Abdeckung, die wirtschaftliche Ergänzung zu dem Verteidigungsteil. Insofern kann man sagen, dass die europäische Entwicklung zunächst einmal ein Kind des Kalten Krieges war, genauso wie die NATO. Und wenn Sie sich heute ansehen, was daraus geworden ist, dann müssen Sie sagen: Das ist ein Wunder. Aus der europäischen Entwicklung ist ein Ding geworden für sich selbst, ein Phänomen, wenn man so will, das aus eigenem Recht etwas geschaffen hat, was damals überhaupt nicht intendiert war, gar nicht gedacht werden konnte. Wir haben keinen völkerrechtlichen Begriff für diese europäische Union, die daraus geworden ist; sie hat zweifelsfrei souveräne Rechte übertragen bekommen von den einzelnen Staaten, sie ist handlungsfähig, aber nicht souverän als einzelne *entity, international entity*, also: Die Gelehrten müssen noch danach suchen, was das ist, aber das werden sie auch noch finden, ist ja auch im Augenblick nicht so wichtig. Dies alles wäre ohne Jean Monnet nicht möglich gewesen, und nicht ohne die Leute, die er von der Richtigkeit einer europäischen Bewegung überzeugt hat.

Der nächste Punkt, an den ich mich erinnere, ist eine verpasste Gelegenheit, nämlich 1954, als es um die EVG ging, die Europäische Verteidigungsgemeinschaft. Wenn die Europäische Verteidigungsgemeinschaft, die ursprünglich von Frankreich vorgeschlagen worden ist, zu Stande gekommen wäre, dann wäre die europäische Entwicklung ganz anders verlaufen. Denn die Europäische Verteidigungsgemeinschaft sollte eine europäische Armee schaffen, das heißt die volle Integration des Sektors Verteidigung, und damit natürlich etwas, wovon wir heute noch träumen. Und es bis heute nicht geschafft haben.

Die Entwicklung wäre völlig anders verlaufen, wir wären viel weiter. Die Franzosen haben es damals vorgeschlagen unter dem Gesichtspunkt: ‚Wenn es schon nicht zu verhindern ist, dass die Bundesrepublik Deutschland bewaffnet wird, dann wollen wir sie jedenfalls kontrollieren. Und kontrollieren kann man sie am besten, indem man eine Armee schafft ohne deutschen Oberbefehl, sondern unter europäischem Oberbefehl.' Die Franzosen haben diese Idee selber kaputt gemacht, deshalb weil bestimmte rechte Kreise in Frankreich, aber nicht nur die ‚Nein' gesagt haben. Es traf sich, dass ich bei der Sitzung in der französischen Kammer anwesend war, in der der alte Edouard Herriot – sozialistischer Ministerpräsident, saß unmittelbar vor mir und wackelte mit den Händen, mit dem Blatt gegen das Mikrophon – sagte: „Wenn es denn wieder sein sollte, dass wir die Söhne Frankreichs zu den Waffen rufen müssen, um uns zu verteidigen, dann werden sie bereit sein, für Frankreich zu sterben, aber nicht für Europa."

Das war 1954. Wenn Sie eine Sekunde daran denken, mit welchen Argumenten jetzt auch das, was man den Verfassungsvertrag nennt, abgelehnt worden ist, das heißt: mit dem Widerstand gegen die Übertragung von Souveränitäten, durch die die nationale Souveränität beeinträchtigt wird, dann sehen Sie, dass allen ungeheuren Entwicklungen zum Trotz bestimmte Grundhaltungen der europäischen Nationen, insbesondere einer so stolzen wie Frankreich, sich nur bedingt und langsam verändert haben.

1960 und folgende Jahre haben wir dann also eine Entwicklung gehabt, in der es langsam voran ging mit der Erweiterung der Kompetenzen über Kohle und Stahl hinaus, im Prinzip war das auch in Deutschland gar nicht umstritten. Im Prinzip war nur wichtig: Die europäische

Egon Bahr

Entwicklung sollte uns nicht daran hindern, wenn möglich die deutsche Einheit zu fördern. Sollte also die deutsche Einheit nicht blockieren.

Als Willy Brandt 1969 Bundeskanzler wurde, hat er als seine erste außenpolitische Aktion sich getroffen, in Den Haag, mit Pompidou und den anderen. Und es gelang, für Großbritannien den Weg in die Gemeinschaft zu öffnen. Pompidou hat das wahrscheinlich auch gemacht unter dem Gesichtspunkt, also wenn die Deutschen nun anfangen, Ostpolitik zu machen, wer weiß, was dabei rauskommt, dann wäre es gar nicht so schlecht, wenn wir nicht allein mit den Deutschen sind, sondern die Engländer auch dabei sind. Deshalb hat er die Blockierung Großbritanniens, durch de Gaulle, aufgehoben. Für Brandt ging es um etwas anderes. Brandt war der Auffassung: Es kann der europäischen Entwicklung gar nicht schaden, im Gegenteil es kann ihr nur nützen, wenn die englischen und skandinavischen demokratischen Erfahrungen und Elemente hineinkommen. Er war von allem Anfang an für die Einbeziehung sowohl Großbritanniens wie der skandinavischen Staaten.

Das ist dann also geschehen, wobei ich hinzufügen möchte, dass Brandt später enttäuscht war und gesagt hat: „Vielleicht hatte de Gaulle doch recht, die Engländer nicht dabei haben zu wollen. Vielleicht ist es doch richtig, dass Großbritannien seine *special relationship* zu Amerika höher schätzt als seine europäischen Neigungen oder seine europäischen Bereitschaften." Aber ich komme darauf zurück, denn bis dahin ging alles noch in der Konstellation der Sechs, die dann durch Großbritannien erweitert wurde.

Als wir dann die Verhandlungen mit der Sowjetunion aufnahmen zu dem, was später zum Moskauer Vertrag von 1970 wurde, erinnere ich sehr genau, an einen schönen Februartag 1970, als zum ersten Mal der sowjetische Außenminister, Gromyko, die deutsche Botschaftsresidenz besuchte und mittags was zu essen bekam. Und nach dem Essen haben wir unseren Kaffee balanciert. Und er fragte mich: „Wann muss man damit rechnen, dass Europa mit einer Stimme spricht?" Darauf habe ich ihm gesagt: „Wiedervorlage in 20 Jahren, Herr Minister." Darauf hat er gesagt: „Meinen Sie das ehrlich?" – „Ja." Dann kam ich zurück und habe das dem Bundeskanzler berichtet, und daraufhin sagte er: „Du bist ein Defätist".

Ich kann das deshalb nicht vergessen, weil nun 35 Jahre vergangen sind, und Europa immer noch das Ziel hat, mit einer Stimme sprechen zu wollen. Es geht zum Verzweifeln langsam, und ich wäre wirklich froh, wenn das, sagen wir mal, in fünf Jahren gelingen würde, aber

Europa 1945 und Heute

daran kann man zweifeln. Das heißt, es fehlt bei allem, was dazu gekommen ist, an Kompetenzen, sogar an Kompetenzen, was die Währung angeht, den Euro also. Der Durchbruch zur Handlungsfähigkeit international gelingt nur durch entsprechenden Souveränitätsverzicht auf den Gebieten der Außen- und Sicherheitspolitik. Die berühmte Telefonnummer, die Henry Kissinger angemahnt hat, ohne sie zu vermissen natürlich, „wen kann er anrufen, wenn er mit Europa sprechen will?" Das gilt immer noch. Denn das was also dazukommen sollte, wenigstens ein kleines Schrittchen in diese Richtung, durch diesen europäischen Verfassungsvertrag mit einem europäischen Außenminister, das ist nun auch für eine unbestimmte Zeit vorbei. Man kann nicht damit rechnen, wann und ob der europäische Verfassungsvertrag wiederbelebt werden kann.

In diesem Zusammenhang sollte man sich vielleicht klar machen, dass die gesamte europäische Entwicklung etwas gewesen ist, was von verbaler Hochstapelei begleitet war. Wir haben dieses Ding Gemeinschaft, also EG, genannt, als sie das noch gar nicht war. Sie sollte erst etwas werden. Weil man nichts Besseres zu tun hatte, oder einem nichts Besseres einfiel, hat man das ganze dann „Europäische Union" genannt. Es war aber keine Union. Es sollte erst eine werden.

So. Und der Gipfel war, dass man zum Schluss einen europäischen Verfassungsvertrag gemacht hat, der keine Verfassung bedeutete. Denn wenn das angenommen worden wäre, hätte ja niemand seine Verfassung ändern müssen. Kein Mitgliedstaat. Das heißt, Europa hat immer ein bisschen mehr in seiner eigenen Titulatur und in seinen Ansprüchen gefordert, als es fähig war zu realisieren.

Jetzt kommt ein anderer Faktor hinzu, und zwar der tiefe Einschnitt, der geschichtlich tiefe Einschnitt, das Ende der Teilung; der Teilung Europas, der Teilung Deutschlands, der Teilung Berlins. Wir haben als Europäer immer gesagt, wir halten den Platz offen für die europäischen Völker im Osteuropa. Wenn sie denn kommen können und frei sind und auch kommen wollen. So, das ist jetzt der Fall.

So schrecklich begeistert waren die Westeuropäer nicht darüber. Aber wir haben uns selbstverständlich an das Wort gehalten, und es ist ja auch historisch richtig; es ist ja historisch nötig. Es ist eine ungeheure Chance, eine Einheit Europas zu schaffen unter den Gesichtspunkten der EU. Ich sage ja gerade nichts von der NATO, denn zu den Wundern der EU gehört ja, dass ihre Mitglieder untereinander nicht mehr kriegsfähig sind. Es ist ja nicht nur der

Egon Bahr

Traum wahr geworden, dass es keinen Krieg mehr zwischen Deutschland und Frankreich geben kann. Sondern kein Land innerhalb der EU kann ein anderes Land innerhalb der EU bekriegen. Wenn es nur die EU gäbe auf der Welt, brauchten die europäischen Staaten überhaupt keine Streitkräfte mehr. Bekanntlich ist dem nicht so; deshalb brauchen wir auch Streitkräfte. Aber gut.

Wir haben die Illusion gehabt, die Erweiterung zugleich mit der Vertiefung erreichen zu können. Vertiefung hieß also die Sache regierbar machen. Erweiterung hieß, jeder, der die Voraussetzungen erfüllt, kann Mitglied der EU werden. Jetzt haben wir fünfundzwanzig. Wir werden wahrscheinlich 2007/2008 zwei weitere dazu bekommen, Rumänien und Bulgarien, das sind dann siebenundzwanzig. Als die EG sechs Mitglieder hatte, waren wir nicht im Stande, eine gemeinsame Nahostpolitik zu entwickeln. Als das dann neun wurden – auch nicht. Als das zwölf wurden – auch nicht. Als das fünfzehn wurden – auch nicht. Mit fünfundzwanzig bin ich sehr skeptisch, ob es da leichter wird. Mit siebenundzwanzig noch mehr.

Das heißt, ein wesentlicher Punkt ist die Frage, wie kriegt man dieses Riesending „handhabbar" und also regierungsfähig? Das ist einer der wesentlichen Punkte des sogenannten Verfassungsvertrages. Ob der scheitert oder wiederbelebt werden kann, ist im Augenblick völlig wurscht. Die Frage wie man das System der fünfundzwanzig zum Arbeiten bringt ohne zu große Reibungsverluste, muss in jedem Falle gelöst werden. Notfalls müssen die Teile herausgelöst werden aus dem Verfassungsvertrag, um jedenfalls die Sache regierungsfähig zu machen.

Ich bin hierher gekommen auch unter dem Gesichtspunkt: Europa hat seine Selbstbestimmung verlangt noch während des Kalten Krieges. Die europäische Selbstbestimmung während des Kalten Krieges war natürlich eine wirtschaftliche. Eine militärische konnte sie ja nicht sein. Denn militärisch waren wir von der Garantie der Amerikaner abhängig. Das ist nun anders. Zum ersten Mal seit dem Ende des Zweiten Weltkriegs ist durch den Zusammenbruch der Sowjetunion und des Warschauer Pakts eine Lage entstanden, in der Europa nicht mehr bedroht ist – militärisch. Russland ist schwach, ungeheuer schwach. Zum ersten Mal lebt Russland nicht mehr in sicheren, unangetasteten Grenzen. Russland ist gerade in der Lage, nehme ich an – auf dem einzigen Sektor, auf dem es mit den Amerikanern noch reden kann und ernst genommen wird – die atomare Zweitschlagsfähigkeit zu erhalten. Aber jedenfalls konventionell – und konventionell ist das einzige worüber Europa reden kann – für die europäische Union gibt es keine Bedrohung mehr. Wir brauchen Amerika zu unserer konventionellen Verteidigung nicht mehr. Europa kann anfangen, auch auf sicherheitspolitischem Gebiet selbstbestimmend zu werden. Und das erste Mal, in dem Europa das zeigte, war als es um den Irakkrieg ging, als eine Reihe europäischer Länder nicht an die Seite von Washington getreten sind, sondern die europäische Option genommen haben.

Das ist für mich eine Sache, in der ich den gegenwärtigen Kanzler[1] in eine Reihe stelle – mit Adenauer, der die Westbindung gemacht hat; mit Brandt, der die Öffnung nach Osten gemacht hat; mit Kohl, der den Instinkt und den Mut hatte, die Einheit zu machen bzw. zuzugreifen, als die Gelegenheit sich bot. Gerhard Schröder hat die europäische Option auch in sicherheitspolitischen Fragen mit der daraus folgenden Emanzipation von Amerika geschafft. Wobei wir natürlich keine Sekunde übersehen können, wie lieb es Amerika ist, wenn Europa sich nicht so schnell vereinigt. Es ist dann viel leichter zu manipulieren. Und natürlich sind zwanzig oder fünfundzwanzig leichter zu beeinflussen als eine außenpolitische Einheit. Und wir haben das ja erlebt, dieser berühmte Brief der Acht zur Unterstützung der USA ist in Washington entworfen worden.[2] Und ist dann über Herrn Aznar an die anderen verteilt worden, und dann hatten wir plötzlich acht europäische Staaten, die sich an die Seite Amerikas, jedenfalls nicht mehr an die Seite von Frankreich und Deutschland und Russland stellten in Sachen Irak. Obwohl die Bevölkerungen in Europa ein europäisches Selbstgefühl hatten und einen europäischen Instinkt hatten, denn die größten Kundgebungen gegen die Irakbeteiligung gab es in London, in Warschau, in Rom und in Madrid. Und in dem Augenblick in dem sich eine Gelegenheit bot, wurde in Madrid sogar die Regierung dementsprechend abgewählt.

Das heißt für mich: Wird Europa in der Lage sein, auch militärisch, sicherheitspolitisch, handlungsfähig und selbstbestimmt zu sein? Das ist jedenfalls das Ziel, das sich Europa gesetzt hat und das auf vielen Konferenzen beschworen, beschlossen, unterstrichen worden ist. Das bedeutet eine Lage zu ändern, die Zbigniew Brzezinski, Sicherheitsberater von Präsident Jimmy Carter, in einem bemerkenswerten Buch nach dem tiefen Einschnitt – Ende der Sowjetunion und des War-

---

[1] Gerhard Schröder (SPD). (Anm. des Herausgebers.)
[2] Im Januar 2003 hatten die Regierungschefs Großbritanniens, Italiens, Spaniens, Portugals, Ungarns, Polens, Dänemarks und der Tschechei ihre Unterstützung der US-Position in den diplomatischen Auseinandersetzungen im Vorfeld des Irak-Krieges zu erkennen gegeben. (Anm. des Herausgebers.)

schauer Pakts – so beschrieben hat: „Amerika ist nun die einzige Supermacht. Die einzige Supermacht muss dafür sorgen, dass der euroasiatische Kontinent unter unserer Kontrolle bleibt, kontrollierbar bleibt." Er macht dann bestimmte Bemerkungen zu Japan, zu China, zu Indien, zu Indonesien, zum Mittleren Osten, zum Nahen Osten, und dann kommt er auf Europa und sagt: "Europa ist unser Protektorat."

Sicherheitspolitisch ist Europa ein amerikanisches Protektorat. Und die Frage, ob es das bleiben will, oder ob es seinen Beschlüssen folgen will, ist für mich offen. Genauer gesagt, hat Großbritannien Europa vor diese Frage gestellt, oder vor diese Entscheidung jetzt gestellt. Der gegenwärtige Ratsvorsitzende, Tony Blair, hat mit der ganzen ihm eigenen Beredsamkeit für die wundervollen Perspektiven des Wohlstands in einem gemeinsamen Markt geworben, ohne auch nur zu begründen, warum er das politische Ziel Europa ablehnt. Er nennt Europäische Union, was nur die Hälfte dessen ist, was die Europäische Union beschlossen hat. Die andere Häfte, die internationale Handlungsfähigkeit, fehlt völlig.

Es handelt sich dabei, nach meiner Beurteilung, um die Fortsetzung der englischen Politik gegenüber Europa in den ganzen letzten fünfzig Jahren. Ich habe mit Interesse, wie Sie sich vorstellen können, vor kurzem in den Erinnerungen von George Kennan gelesen der 1949 Planungschef im State Department war und damals Europa besucht hat um festzustellen: Kann man die europäische Einigung mit dem Blick auf Gesamteuropa unternehmen, ohne in das militärische Denken oder in den Vorrang des militärischen Denkens abzugleiten? Er schreibt also in seinen Erinnerungen, und ich zitiere: "Die Abneigung der Briten gegen einen Beitritt zu einer kontinentalen Union schien mir so zwingend zu sein, dass eine europäische Bewegung, an der sie sich beteiligten, es nie sehr weit bringen würde. Sie würde den organisatorischen Zusammenschluss nie in das Stadium eines wirklichen Suveränitätsverzichts gelangen lassen". Ich kann nur sagen, George Kennan hatte damals recht, und er hat bis heute recht behalten. Ob konservative oder Labour-Premierminister: Die traditionellen Sonderbeziehungen zwischen London und Washington haben den Vorzug behalten. Die Abneigung gegen eine politische Union wurde zielgerecht verfolgt, mal etwas brutaler, mal eleganter, mal als Bremser, mal als Teilnehmer, um besser bremsen und kontrollieren zu können. Immer für die Erweiterung – eine riesige Erweiterung natürlich, auch mit der Türkei und Georgien und ich weiß nicht was, weil die Erweiterung die politische Einheit erschwert und das mit Washington abgestimmte Gewicht Londons erhalten würde.

Ich kann das verstehen im Interesse Großbritanniens, kritisiere das gar nicht. Ich sage nur: Europa darf sich nicht bremsen lassen durch London. Wenn Europa entschlossen gewesen ist, ist London im letzten Augenblick immer auf den fahrenden Zug gesprungen. Auf Dauer wird auch Großbritannien nicht darum herumkommen, sich zu entscheiden, ob es die Europäische Union mit der beschlossenen politischen Selbstbestimmung mitmachen will, oder ob es sie keinesfalls mitmachen will. So lange Europa Großbritannien nicht vor diese Frage stellt, wird Europa die internationale Handlungsfähigkeit nicht erreichen, weil London in der bequemen Lage der letzten vierzig Jahre bleiben kann. Dann wird Europa als sicherheitspolitisches Protektorat, als großer gemeinsamer Markt die Aufgabe behalten, wirtschaftspolitisch die Erweiterungen der NATO zu unterstützen, den Lebensstandard der neuen Mitglieder der NATO zu heben, ohne seine eigenen Interessen verfolgen zu können. Die müssen nicht immer deckungsgleich mit den amerikanischen sein, gerade nicht in der Region des Nahen und Mittleren Ostens, auf die sich das strategische Interesse der USA zu Recht richtet.

Nach dem brillanten amerikanischen militärischen Sieg im Irak haben sich alle europäischen politischen Bedenken über die Folgen bestätigt und zu dem Ergebnis geführt, dass Europa natürlich helfen muss, dass Amerika aus einem Desaster herauskommt, das es selbst verursacht hat. Gegenüber dem Iran könnte sich Ähnliches entwickeln. Weil Europa nicht handlungsfähig gewesen ist, war es unfähig, Amerika vor den Folgen seines Angriffskrieges ohne UN-Mandat zu bewahren, den es wahrscheinlich gegenüber einer geschlossenen europäischen Haltung nicht unternommen hätte. Wenn Europa nicht zur politischen Geschlossenheit findet, kann es geschichtlich mitschuldig werden an der Entwicklung einer explosiven Region in Zentral-Asien, die dann praktisch allein von den Interessen Washingtons bestimmt würde. Europa würde sich selbst zu einem global entbehrlichen Faktor degradieren. Das wäre letztlich die Folge, falls Europa Großbritannien nicht vor die erwähnte entscheidende Frage stellt.

Der gegenwärtige Zustand Europas ist enttäuschend. Frankreich ist mit dem Blick aud die Wahlen 2007 gelähmt. Polen kokettiert mit dem Gedanken, der verlässlichste Verbündete Amerikas zu werden. Über Italien braucht man nicht zu reden.[3] Die neue deutsche Regierung wird

---

[3] Der damalige italienische Regierungschef Silvio Berlusconi hatte sich im irakischen Krieg völlig auf die Seite der USA gestellt. (Anm. des Herausgebers.)

Egon Bahr

die Kontinuität für Europa und überhaupt außenpolitisch mit der Vorgänger-Regierung fortsetzen, findet aber dafür keinen entsprechenden Partner. Die Frage, ob Europa also die Kraft finden wird, außenpolitisch selbstbestimmt zu werden, ist gegenwärtig nicht zu beantworten.

September 2005

CHAPTER 2

'OLD IDEAS IN NEW BODIES'

The Economic Reconstruction of Europe in 1945

Patricia Clavin

The contrast between the two eras after the First and Second World War was striking. In the twenty years that followed the First World War, Europe was bedevilled by crises, economic, political and diplomatic, yet the twenty years that followed the Second World War were the most prosperous and stable of the twentieth century. By 1952 not only had Western Europe recovered from the war, but national economies continued to grow at an average rate of seven per cent a year for the next ten years. Europe of the 1920s and 1930s, by contrast, never truly recovered from the war, a comparison rendered all the more striking because the economic costs of fighting the Second World War were far greater than the first. Much more was spent on waging war, more property and infrastructure lay in ruins and, on a global scale, many more people had lost their lives through war than in the First World War. Across the world around 60 million people died.

When it comes to the historiography of European reconstruction, much of the early historical work focused on the contribution of the United States. This preoccupation was shaped partly by the origins of the Cold War and partly by the way in which the Second World War had enhanced American power and weakened Europe. Among the war's participants, the United States alone suffered negligible human and physical losses. America was now, in absolute and relative terms, wealthier and stronger than it had ever been before. During the war its gross national product had more than doubled and, in sharp contrast to

1919, it enjoyed the military muscle, diplomatic expertise and political will for intervention in international affairs.[1]

After 1940, the United States attempted to provide the leadership and policies to shape the reconstruction of Europe that had been so desperately absent in 1919. In common with their European counterparts, American policy-makers and advisors were determined to learn the lessons of the interwar period. In June 1941, the point was underlined when President Roosevelt announced that the Atlantic Charter, the blue print of principles for postwar co-operation, was to ensure that 'tragic mistakes shall not be made again'.[2] This preoccupation with the lessons of history was unsurprising given the spectacular failure of the domestic economies in the face of the Great Depression that ravaged free market capitalism, liberal democracy and international co-operation after 1929. These crises helped to generate a sustained determination on the part of the American government to set up institutions to safeguard, not only international peace, but monetary stability and economic co-operation.

One of the key lessons drawn by the Americans from the Great Depression, reinforced by its experience as an Allied power in the Second World War, was the value of consistent international co-operation. This, the Americans believed was best sustained and protected within international institutions. Much of the early American planning for postwar Europe focused on designing institutions that were to become the International Bank for Reconstruction and Development (IBRD), otherwise known as the World Bank, the International Monetary Fund and a proposed World Trade Organisation. America also encouraged revised forms of regional co-operation in Europe, too, that supported initiatives taken by future architects of European Union such as Jean Monnet. For much of Europe's new-found will for economic co-operation emerged independently, not just of American influence, but state influence altogether among western European businessmen. This group also facilitated transnational connections between European and American industry through which European businessmen, in many

---

[1] Key texts on America's new appetite for international leadership include: Warren Kimball, *The Juggler, Franklin D Roosevelt as Wartime Statesman* (Princeton University Press: New York, 1991); Thomas Zeiler, *Free Trade. Free World* (University of North Carolina, Chapel Hill, 1999); John L Harper, *American Visions of Europe* (Cambridge U.P, Cambridge, 1996).

[2] 'Christmas Eve Fireside Chat on Teheran and Cairo Conferences, 24 December 1943' in S.I. Rosenman (ed.), *The Public Papers and Addresses of Franklin D. Roosevelt* (New York, 1950), p. 559.

ways, demonstrated a new enthusiasm for the process of Americanization begun in the first half of the twentieth century.

Indeed, recent writing on the economic reconstruction of postwar Europe has stressed that the early wellsprings of Western Europe's spectacular recovery after the war were located in the domestic economy. Not only did the Second World War bequeath beneficial economic legacies for the largest economies in Europe, governments had tested new tools with which to stabilize and facilitate growth in the domestic economy. The Second World War had triggered significant levels of industrial investment: Britain, France, Italy, the USSR and Germany all finished the war with higher stocks of machine tools than before the war had begun. (In Germany's case the level of industrial investment was so high it effectively countered the impact of Allied bombing on the economy.) These increased levels of domestic investment were sustained after the war and were substantially higher than in the interwar period.[3] So, too, was industry's commitment to research and development and to exploiting the amount and reliability of statistical information available on the performance of the economy. Economic science had received a huge fillip from the Second World War; there were many more trained economists employed in government and industry during and after it than before 1939.

Much scientific and business expertise was shared across frontiers – academic and business exchange schemes became commonplace after the Second World War – and underlines that the second postwar era was distinguished by a new balance between the national and the international. If the IMF, the IBRD and the General Agreement on Trade and Tariffs were not important to the first ten years of European reconstruction, they became significant to the expansion of international trade and exchange in subsequent decades; as did the new institutions of European economic and social co-operation, notably the European Economic Community.

So while the early emphasis on European economic reconstruction was on the role played by the United States, new research emphasises the degree to which western Europe was the author of its own recovery. Indeed, it is possible to take the argument one step further, for Europe's critique of American 'irresponsibility' in the inter-war period, articulated also by institutions like the League of Nations, helped to reshape American foreign economic policy after war's end.

---

[3] Barry Eichengreen, *The European Economy Since 1945. Coordinated Capitalism and Beyond* (2007), pp. 86-130.

Patricia Clavin

A crucial, but hitherto neglected element in facilitating intra-European economic co-operation and American 'education' on a host of levels, was the Economic and Financial Organisation (EFO) of the League of Nations. During the 1930s EFO became the largest and most active element of the League, facilitating intellectual and practical co-operation on a wide range of issues. Primary material production, trade practises, the operation of the gold standard and the impact of Nazi-style economics on Europe were just a few of the topics it addressed.

Of course, categorizing an organisation that was intended to pioneer international co-operation on a global scale as one that worked primarily to facilitate intra-European relations is not unproblematic. But in many ways EFO, and the League as a whole, was a very European institution located at the heart of Europe. Although sixty-one countries eventually joined (but not the United States), the League was dominated by European powers and their pre-occupations: Britain and France provided its leadership while many of the permanent and non-permanent members of the Council of the League of Nations were European. Much of its work in the 1920s and 1930s was focused on Europe – the reconstruction of the Central and Eastern Europe, its concern for the minorities question triggered by the collapse of European Empires and re-drawing of central and eastern European borders. Its work in the field of disarmament was, again, primarily centred on Europe. Its social and physical space, too, was European – the purpose built *Palais des Nations* in Geneva – as were the League's official languages (French and English) and the habits that governed its diplomacy. Of the 55 League members in 1928, 26 of them were European, contributing around 65 per cent of the total budget. (Britain alone contributed over 10 per cent and France around 7 per cent.) When the personnel composition of the League is taken into account, the dominance of European countries is even more striking, with the smaller nations, in particular, offering the League intellectual thrust, enthusiasm and commitment.

By 1945, the year in which it was succeeded by the United Nations and the Bretton Woods institutions, EFO had amassed over twenty-five years worth of skill in the field of international economic and financial relations, drawing into its orbit a huge range of divergent expertise from around the world (although predominately from Europe) which had been sustained by a regular and diverse programme of meetings and a voluminous publication record.⁴ In 1927 and 1933 the Committee sponsored World Economic Conferences that sought to facilitate co-operation on almost every major economic and financial issue facing the modern world. It produced a number of key reports annually, the most important of which included a *Statistical Yearbook of the League of Nations* and *The World Economic Survey*. Single issue studies, equally, made a big impact, including Gottfried Harberler's *Prosperity and Depression. A Theoretical Analysis of Cyclical Movements* published in 1936.⁵ Perhaps even more impressive was the quality and number of economists who worked for EFO. The roll call read like a *Who's Who* of leading twentieth-century economists, including the Swedish economist Bertil Ohlin, the Dutchman Tjalling Koopmans, the American Jacob Viner, the Austrians Gottfried Harberler and Wilhelm Röpke, the Estonian/Canadian Ragnar Nurkse and the Briton James Meade. Their contribution was varied, but all participated in the work of EFO's Depression Delegation that began in 1938, their number swollen by an additional 17 economists. Prior to the Second World War, EFO served as both actor and stage in international economic and financial relations with many of the themes that shaped its contribution to post-war planning and reconstruction already well established.

In 1939, the outbreak of the war marked the final, ignominious failure of the League of Nations as an agency by which international peace might be secured. When it came to the League's work in the field of peace and disarmament, historians generally date the failure much earlier with the collapse of the Disarmament Conference in 1933, while in the contemporary mind, the League slumped to an all-time low with its inability to offer effective support and protection to Abyssinia (Ethiopia) in 1935.⁶ The League's failure to preserve peace, its public *raison d'être*, redoubled the United States' determination to

---

⁴ Patricia Clavin and Jens-Wilhelm Wessels, 'Transnationalism and the League of Nations: Understanding the Work of its Economic and Financial Organisation', *Contemporary European History*. Vol. 14,4 (2005) pp. 465-492; Pierre-Yves Gherbali, 'The League of Nations and Functionalism', in A.J.R. Groom and Paul Taylor (Ed.s) *Functionalism. Theory and Practice in International Relations* (London, 1975).

⁵ Gottfried Harberler, *Prosperity and Depression. A Theoretical Analysis of Cyclical Movements* (first edition, League of Nations: Geneva, 1936).

⁶ Although Andrew Webster has drawn out how the League generated a shared expertise in how to effect disarmament that had a productive impact on international relations in the longer run. See Andrew Webster, 'The Transnational Dream: Politicians, Diplomats and Soldiers in the League of Nations' Pursuit of International Disarmament', 1920-1938, *Contemporary European History*, 14.4, 2005, pp. 493-518.

have little open contact with the institution. The public face of American diplomacy, however, was very different from its private conduct, especially when it came to economics.

During the 1930s, not only had economic issues come to dominate the work of the League of Nations (EFO was by far the largest division of the League), but the Americans were heavily involved in this work. The growing American participation was especially evident in EFO's promotion of an American-authored initiative to reduce international trade restrictions and its support of the 1939 Bruce Committee to restructure EFO. By August 1940 the relationship between EFO and the USA was cemented when the Economic and Financial Organisation moved to Princeton and was soon absorbed into the huge network of experts engaged in planning for the post-war world. EFO's head, the Briton, Alexander Loveday hoped that the Secretariat of EFO would form the core of the secretariat for one or more of the planned new institutions intended to safeguard international co-operation. But this was always a political impossibility for the Americans who were determined to present their post-war diplomacy as a sharp break from the failures of the past. Covertly, however, EFO continued to play an important role in nurturing America's burgeoning appetite for economic internationalism.

Both during and after the Second World War, successive administrations made extensive use of EFO's personnel and publications. The organisation's pre-occupation with planning and the importance of learning the lessons of history chimed with dominant themes in American foreign policy.[7] EFO officials and American representatives shared common beliefs, in particular, the conviction that the *ad hoc* approach to the problem of policy co-ordination after the First World War was responsible for the economic and financial crises that bedevilled Europe and the rest of the world during the inter-war period. Although

---

[7] See EFO's contribution to US investigations into the functions of international organisations. Records of the League of Nations, Geneva (hereafter LN), LN Princeton Office, C1629-C1630, File C.1629-No 1 'Allocation Committee – Reports'; League of Nations, *First Report of the Supervisory Commission for the Year 1943*, Geneva, 20 Sept 1943; Library of Congress, Washington DC, Private Papers of Leo Pasvolsky, Box 7, File 'Post-war Planning, 1942-43', Memoranda entitled 'Enumeration of Some of the New Functions That Have Been Proposed For Universal Organisations', 10 June 1943. LN Princeton Office, C1629-C1630, File C. 1629 No 1 (1) 21-45, 'Discussions of Financial Problems of UNRRA', 30 August 1943. George Woodbridge, *UNRRA: The History of the United Nations Relief and Rehabilitation Administration,* Vols. 1&2 (New York, Columbia University Press, 1950).

conditions for EFO were far from ideal (for one thing money was very tight), its officials remained very busy throughout the war. They churned out a huge range of reports and plans that were disseminated widely, met a great many senior representatives from the American agencies involved in post-war planning and reconstruction – Foreign Economic Administration (FEA), various State Department committees, the Research and Analysis Branch of the Office of Strategic Services (OSS), the US Treasury, advisors to the White House, and the Board of the Federal Reserve in New York – and leading figures from Britain and governments in exile from occupied Europe.[8]

Much of EFO's wartime work and postwar contribution grew out of the extensive work of the Delegation on Economic Depressions which had begun in 1937 and continued throughout the war. When it came to the shared beliefs of EFO members, two themes, in particular, stood out. The first reflected a pre-occupation with developing an internationally-shared notion of the conditions that would generate and sustain economic stability in the longer term economic policy. This was set out in a lengthy report entitled, *Economic Stability in the Post-War World* published in 1945 and was supplemented by an additional thirteen published studies. These included: *Agricultural Production in Continental Europe during the 1914-1918 War and Reconstruction Period* (1943), *The International Currency Experience. Lessons of the Inter-War Period* (1944), *Europe's Trade. A Study of the Trade of European Countries with Each Other and with the Rest of the World* (1941) and *Europe's Overseas Needs and How They Were Met* (1943).

The second theme that emerged in EFO's wartime discussions with American planners was the more immediate programme question of how Europe would manage *The Transition from War to Peace* economy, and a publication on this topic appeared in 1943.[9] All EFO's ma-

---

[8] Other contacts included the British Embassy in Washington, the Foreign Office, the British Treasury, Board of Trade and Ministry of Economic Warfare, the Cabinet Offices and the Bank of England. They also had extensive contacts to Canada, including the Canadian Finance Ministry and the Central Bank, as well as assorted think tanks, notably Council of Foreign Relations, the Institute for International Relations (Chatham House). For details of its programme of work, see LN Princeton Office, C 1624, File C. 1624-No 3 42-46, 'Section Meetings'. For details of its financial worries, see League of Nations, *First Report of the Supervisory Commission for the Year 1943* (Geneva, 1943), pp. 8-9; LN Princeton Office, C1629-C1630, File C. 1629, No. 121-43, 'Allocation Committee - Reports'.

[9] *Economic Stability in the Post-War World. The Conditions of Prosperity after the Transition from War to Peace*. Report of the Delegation on Economic Depressions, Part II, (League of Nations, Geneva, 1945); *The Transition from War to Peace Economy*, Report of the Delegation on Economic Depressions, Part I (League of

jor publications and supplementary reports articulated deeply held convictions regarding the means by which, in particular, European reconstruction should be effected at war's end: first and foremost was the conviction that planning and communication of information between nations was crucial – the hyperinflation and depression which blighted interwar Europe were eloquent demonstrations of what could happen again if this was ignored. Closer European economic integration was an adjunct of this EFO worldview and it was encouraged to undertake an extensive study of the subject by a former EFO advisor Jean Monnet in 1943 and 1944.[10] Equally important was the conviction that structural changes within the world's economy (although the evidence base on which EFO drew was predominately European), had made modern economies much more prone to depression than ever before. These changes included the increasing consumption of durable goods as well as the fact that labour costs had grown more rigid, and EFO believed that these structural changes were likely to have been exacerbated by war and occupation.

The organisation offered a four-pronged policy response to these longer-term challenges that found a loud echo in the policies adopted by the United States both at the Bretton Woods negotiations and during the immediate post-war years. Firstly, there should be a continued, and preferably institutionalised, exchange and development of expertise and information on how best to manage the domestic economy. Secondly, multilateral trade links to liberate international trade should be extensively promoted. This view, again, was echoed in the planned

---

Nations, Geneva, 1943). It seems unlikely these reports were published in Geneva and then shipped to the enormous distribution list which included all of the Americas, governments in neutral counties or those with good relations with the Allies, including representatives of all governments in exile. Rather, it is likely that all these materials were printed in Washington DC. Both parts of the report were associated with a large number of other League publications. Part I made reference to reports entitled: *Relief Deliveries and Relief Loans, 1919-1923* (League of Nations: Geneva, 1943), *Europe's Overseas Needs, 1919-1920 and How They Were Met* (League of Nations: Geneva, 1943), *Economic Fluctuations in the United States and the United Kingdom, 1918-1922* (League of Nations: Geneva, 1943), *Agricultural Production in Continental Europe During the 1914-1918 War and the Reconstruction Period* (League of Nations: Geneva, 1943). Part II drew on: *The Network of World Trade, Commercial Policy in the Interwar Period: International Proposals and National Policies* (League of Nations: Geneva, 1942), *Trade Relations Between Free-Market and Controlled Economies*, and *Quantitative Trade Controls: Their Causes and Natures* (League of Nations: Geneva, 1943).

[10] Economic and Financial Committees, *Report to the Council on the Work of the 1943 Joint Session, Princeton, N.J* 1943 (published February 1944), pp. 15-20.

International Trade Organisation and in the eventual General Agreement on Trade and Tariffs, although, significantly, EFO officials believed the European countries might require a little more time than the United States Trade and State Departments might like before they would be ready to open their economies to 'free trade' at war's end.

A third theme in EFO's message to American policy-makers, later rehearsed in a variety of ways in American policy, was its view that the world's richer countries need to act responsibly with regard to the poorer ones in the framing of international economic and financial policy. This was primarily articulated in a call for generous but responsible lending by creditors while allowing the world's debtors to retain trade and currency controls as long as they were needed to aid reconstruction. Although this was not immediately apparent in American internationalism in 1945, in part because the Americans had underestimated the challenge before them in Europe, EFO's view found a clear echo in the European Recovery Plan announced by George Marshall in 1947. The final strand of EFO's plan for economic reconstruction supported the call for fixed but flexible exchange rates in financial policy. Born of years of study in the 1930s, combined with behind-the-scenes involvement in the negotiations between John Maynard Keynes and Harry Dexter White, EFO officials concluded that this monetary policy was the best way to safeguard financial stability.

When it came to the challenges facing those charged with effecting European reconstruction in the short term, EFO also made an important contribution. By 1943, after a passionate but short-lived rivalry with the International Labour Organisation from which EFO emerged triumphant, the organisation played a crucial role in determining the programme of work for the United Nations Relief and Rehabilitation Administration (UNRRA) and in creating the United Nations Food and Agriculture Organisation.[11]

In both the short and long-term pre-occupations of American planners, EFO was the main provider of intelligence and expertise used by American ministries and agencies when it came to planning post-war relief.[12] In the run-up to the Atlantic City conference in November

---

[11] See, for example, LN Princeton Office, C1170, File C. 1770.No 1 43, Sayre to Loveday, and EFO memoranda, 'Foreign Relief and Rehabilitation – US plans for'; LN Princeton Office, C1629-C1630 No 2, 43, Loveday to Leith-Ross, 22 June 1943.

[12] EFO's statistical contribution to the inter-Allied debate about post-war reparations is an important example. See Patricia Clavin, 'Reparations in the Long Run', *Diplomacy and Statecraft*, Vol. 16, 3 (2005), pp. 515-530.

1943, Loveday and his colleagues regularly attended meetings hosted by the State Department regarding the constitution and focus of UN-RRA. Here the experience of League involvement in the financial and economic reconstruction of central and eastern Europe was especially useful. There were differences between the Americans and the Europeans however. One of the things the League officials sought to impress upon the Americans was that post-war relief measures had to be linked to coherent and considered plans to revitalise the European economies. Short-term planning had to be mindful of longer-term objectives, and in this EFO recommended extending UNRRA's mission to become more than an organisation focused on post-war relief.

At first EFO's plans met with resistance from the Americans and the British but in the end EFO was proved right. The more limited agenda of UNRRA proved inadequate to the tasks before them and, as a result, some of the ideas proposed by EFO that were rejected during the war were revived with the advent of Marshall aid. It is very striking that from 1939 onwards, EFO contended that the only means by which European reconstruction could be successfully effected at the end of the war, was through a real and substantial transfer of resources from the United States to Europe. Indeed, the stability of the new world, it believed, depended on economic stability and prosperity being secured and maintained on a global scale. The argument was made on moral as well as on practical grounds for, as the opening statement on its report regarding *The Transition from War to Peace Economy* made clear, EFO's guiding objective was 'the fullest possible use ... of the resources of production, human and material, of the skill and enterprise of the individual... so as to attain and maintain *in all countries* a stable economy and rising standards of living.'[13]

Both during the 1930s and in the war years, EFO had acted as a clearing-house for intelligence, expertise and experience. Through it, European-based ideas and experience helped to shape the new policies and bodies for Europe made in the USA. The key to EFO's impact was in the range of its governmental as well as non-governmental contacts. These had been cultivated by the inter-governmental elements embedded within the League's organisation. Although the League's ability to generate and disseminate scientific expertise made a path-breaking contribution to the international history of the interwar period, the fact that politicians were required to attend meetings of the Council, the Assembly and assorted sub-committees helped these scientific voices

---

[13] *The Transition from War to Peace Economy*, p. 113.

to be heard. While the League itself may had slid apparently silently into oblivion after 1945, the network of people and ideas it had helped to create lived on well into the post-war years. It shaped amongst other things, European economic reconstruction, international statistical practise, and the new field of what was to become known as 'development economics', which offered a revolutionary new vision of universal economic progress. For the first time all societies of the world had been placed on a single and shared continuum from the least to the most developed, and all were now believed to be on the same path towards a common goal of economic stability and prosperity.

CHAPTER 3

'WITH EUROPE, BUT NOT OF IT'

British Thoughts on Future Anglo-European Relations at the End of the Second World War

Jørgen Sevaldsen

Writers on post-1945 European history very understandably have a tendency to view the years immediately after the defeat of Germany and Italy as a prologue to the Cold War and to the beginnings of European integration. It is refreshing, therefore, to be asked to look at British attitudes and expectations in relation to the Continent in the immediate aftermath of the war, and in the following I intend to be very literal in carrying out this task. I will concentrate on the years 1945-46, i.e. on the situation before the total break-down of relations between the Western powers and the USSR, before the Truman Doctrine (1947) engaged the US in the defence of European democracies, and before the Western European bloc emerged through the Marshall plan (1947) and the formation of the OEEC (1948), the Council of Europe (1949) and NATO (1949). The main focus of the article will be on the academic discussions of the degree of British 'aloofness' from the problems of the Continent in the immediate postwar situation and of possible explanations of this perceived lack of interest in Continental affairs. Did military success in the war make British politicians blind to their country's economic and military weakness and the advisability of concentrating on a European role? Or were they right to concentrate on rebuilding the Commonwealth links and on pursuing a global national strategy?

Jørgen Sevaldsen

The British Position in 1945
The total defeat of Germany in May 1945 and of Japan in August 1945 were seen in Britain as a triumph for British and Allied arms and for the democratic world. There was a feeling of weariness and exhaustion, but also of pride in Britain's part in saving the world from the Nazi and Fascist dictatorships. No Briton could be unaware of the enormous costs of the war – the loss of lives, both as military casualties and as civilian victims of German bombs and rockets, the extensive material damage to towns and cities, and the loss of about a quarter of the national wealth to finance the gigantic war effort. At the same time, most decision-makers at least were quite clear that in terms of resources, Britain was a minor partner in the victorious alliance compared with the USA and the Soviet Union.

Still, there was a general assumption that Britain would continue to be a major world and imperial power and should be acknowledged as such. This feeling might seem unrealistic in retrospect and in the context of later worries about the relative 'decline of Britain' from the 1960s onwards, but historians such as Kenneth O. Morgan have warned against writing Britain off as a great power at this point. In 1945, she was still a major economic and military presence around the world, and she preserved her position as the richest country in Western Europe till the early 1950s.[1] Many authors also note that there was little soul-searching about the national past and the national identity in Britain compared to the situation in most other European countries. As a nation, Britain had nothing to be ashamed of. The war was seen as a triumph of her democratic and gradualist constitutional traditions and as a vindication of Empire. Once again Britain and her global links and interests had been threatened by an autocratic regime on the Continent, and once more Britain had stood up to the challenge.

General Attitudes towards Europe
General British images of Europe before the Second World War had, not surprisingly, included negative as well as positive elements. There is by now a large literature on the way in which British identity was, from the 18th century onwards, shaped by the creation of an opposition between British freedom, Protestantism and commercial peacefulness on the one hand and autocratic French Catholicism and Prussian militarism on the other. In this perspective, Nazism and the Second World War could only confirm the view that the Continent was a dark and

---

[1] Kenneth O. Morgan, *Labour in Power*, Oxford University Press 1984, p. 283.

threatening place. At the same time, Europe also stood for the classical heritage and for impressive achievements in art, music, education and modern science. In 1945, however, the Nazi experience had cast doubts about the whole notion of European civilisation: the revelations in April 1945 of the horrific death camps in the heart of Europe changed irrevocably the historic (and imperial) association of Europe with culture and civilisation. Europe would never be perceived in the same light again after the war, as V.S. Pritchett acknowledged in the *New Statesman* in early 1945:

> *To imagine Europe – that is the hardest thing we have to do. The picture comes to us in fragments and to piece it together and above all hold it in the mind is like trying to hold a dissolving dream and to preserve it from the obstinate platitude of our waking life.*

The postwar problem for Pritchett was one of imagination. The task of reconstruction would encompass not just the slow process of recovering Europe's economic and social structures, but also re-imagining Europe in art and literature in the aftermath of war and mass destruction.[2]

For a Britain which was in 1945 embarking on a period of reconstruction under the leadership of Clement Attlee and his new Labour government, there seemed, however, to be less reason to question the bases of national identity and the democratic culture than there was on the Continent. "The British tended to be witnesses of European *Angst* rather than sharing fully in it."[3]

At the political level, British politicians and officials certainly looked at European problems as representatives of a world power. They realised that Britain had pressing security interests to defend on the Continent and also long-term economic interests in cultivating trade links, but in the chaotic state of the world in 1945, the issues that pressed themselves on decision-makers in London were as often as not non-European problems. If we look, for example, at the detailed ac-

---

[2] John Brannigan, *Literature, Culture and Society in Postwar England 1945-1965*, Lampeter: The Edwin Mellen Press 2002, p. 2. The Pritchett quotation is from the *New Statesman*, vol. xxix, no. 724, 6th January 1945, p. 11. General treatments of Britain's relationship with the Continent include Jens Rahbek Rasmussen and Nils Arne Sørensen, *Briterne og Europa*, Copenhagen: DUPI 1997, and Keith Robbins, *Britain and Europe 1789-2005*, London: Hodder Arnold 2005.

[3] Robbins, op. cit., p. 240.

count of Ernest Bevin's concerns at the Foreign Office in Alan Bullock's biography of the great Labour politician, we will soon realise how global his worries were. There were immediate problems waiting to be solved in the Balkans, in Palestine, Persia, India, China, and Japan. A new world organisation, the United Nations, was being established, and Britain's economic problems vis-à-vis the United States had to be negotiated. Europe was only one corner of the world seen from Whitehall, and the most immediate British tasks there were the organisation of occupation zones in Germany and the feeding of the starving populations in the most war-ravaged parts of the Continent.

As for the longer view, for plans for the future of Europe after the defeat of Germany, it would be fair to say that in the spring of 1945, no official blueprint for a new Europe had been worked out in London.

That does not mean, of course, that no thought had been given to the question. In the early period of the war, Churchill on occasions threw out ideas about a future organisation of Europe based on a Council consisting of representatives of Britain, France, Italy, Spain and 'Prussia', plus of four confederations of smaller states, including a Balkan and a Nordic confederation. Such ideas reflected early plans to reduce Germany to its constituent parts, and also Churchill's view that smaller states were unnatural and generally in the way and ought to co-operate in larger confederations. Later in the war, he talked about a European Council as a regional body within the new United Nations Organisations planned for the postwar period. In the Foreign Office, however, the tendency during 1944-45 was to abandon the idea of dismembering Germany and to move towards accepting that the country would stay unified, but divided into the four occupation zones organised on the lines laid down at the Yalta and Potsdam Conferences in 1945.

In general terms, London's plans in 1945 for maintaining British power and influence in the world may be summarised like this: A United Nations Organisation should be created; war-time co-operation with the USA and Russia should be continued as far as possible; the Commonwealth relationship should be further developed; France should be rebuilt as a guarantee of stability in Western Europe; Germany should be controlled through an occupation regime, a denazification programme, and disarmament, and some form of a Western bloc should be encouraged.

The latter aim was the consequence of a realisation that after Germany's defeat, Britain and the Soviet Union were the only military powers that counted in Europe, and that Britain had an interest in acquiring allies on the Continent. The stark reality was that the British decision-makers were confronted with "the disturbing combination of anxiety about Russian AND uncertainty about American policy".[4]

These anxieties were expressed in a number of position papers from the Foreign Office. Thus, in a celebrated memorandum of 11 July 1945, Orme Sargent, a high-ranking official in the Foreign Office, took stock of Britain's position after victory had been achieved in Western Europe and urged that Britain pursued an independent course between the new superpowers:

> *...because we are numerically the weakest and geographically the smallest of the three Great Powers, it is essential that we should increase our strength in not only the diplomatic but also the economic and military spheres. This clearly can best be done by enrolling the Dominions and especially France, not to mention the lesser Western European Powers, as collaborators with us in this tripartite system. Only so shall we be able, in the long run, to compel our two big partners to treat us as an equal. Even so, our collaboration with the United States and the Soviet Union is not going to be easy in view of the wide divergence between our respective outlooks, traditions and methods...*[5]

Similarly, a Foreign Office brief of 12 July 1945 for the British delegation to the Potsdam Conference stated that small European countries such as Belgium, the Netherlands and Norway were in favour of a Western Group under British leadership, but that the prerequisite for any such development was a Franco-British understanding:

> *... The idea of a 'Western Group' has been suggested in connexion with a 'regional association of Western Europe' within the framework of the World Organisation ... A bilateral Franco-British Treaty of Alliance would provide the foundation and the small Allied countries of North-Western Europe would be attached in some way to the Franco-British Treaty, whether by a multilateral treaty or by arrangements made separately by the*

---

[4] Alan Bullock, *Ernest Bevin. Foreign Secretary 1945-1951*, London: Heinemann 1983, p. 19. The evolution of British policy towards the German question is outlined in Ann Deighton, 'Towards a "Western" Strategy: The Making of British Policy Towards Germany 1945-46', in Ann Deighton, ed., *Britain and the First Cold War*, London: Macmillan 1990, and s.a. *The Impossible Peace. Britain, the Division of Germany and the Origins of the Cold* War, Oxford University Press 1990.
[5] *Documents on British Policy Overseas* I, vol. 1, (HMSO 1984), no. 102.

> *small countries with the United Kingdom and France. The question of admitting to such a system neutrals like Portugal or Sweden would be left to the future ...* [6]

In July 1945, the general election in Britain changed the colour of the Government. The war-time coalition under Churchill's leadership resigned and was replaced by a Labour government under Clement Attlee and with Ernest Bevin as Foreign Secretary. The change of government had important consequences for domestic policies, but not in the field of foreign policy. At a meeting with his officials at the Foreign Office 13 August 1945, Bevin explained that

> *...his long-term policy was to establish close relations between this country and the countries on the Mediterranean and Atlantic fringes of Europe – e.g. more especially Greece, Italy, France, Belgium, the Netherlands and Scandinavia. He wanted to see close association between the United Kingdom and these countries – as much in commercial and economic matters as in political questions. It was necessary to make a start with France, and he was therefore very anxious to put relations between this country and France on to a better footing as soon as possible. As a first step in this direction it seemed essential to endeavour to reach some agreement with the French Government over the question of the Levant ... As regards the further steps to be taken to improve relations with France, the Secretary of State explained that while he was anxious, as he had already said, to work towards a closer association between this country and the countries on the fringe of Europe, more particularly France, he did not wish to take any active steps towards the conclusion of a Franco-British alliance or the formation of a Western group until he had had more time to consider possible Russian reactions ...* [7]

In spite of Bevin's caution regarding Soviet attitudes it is obvious that he was keenly aware of the need to cultivate links with France as well as with the smaller Continental countries. In this context British interests in Scandinavia should not, incidentally, be underestimated. In general, the Nordic region was not a high-profile one seen from the imperial centre in London. Nevertheless, there had been a growing

---

[6] Ibid., no. 119.
[7] *Documents on British Policy Overseas,* I, vol. 5, (HMSO 1990), no. 4.

awareness in Britain in the interwar period that Scandinavia and Britain were linked by shared democratic values and that the Nordic countries were of considerable importance to Britain as trading partners. In 1945, Denmark and to some extent Norway owed their liberation from German occupation largely to the efforts of Field Marshall Montgomery's armies in Northern Germany, and there was an expectation in London that the Nordic region would become a British sphere of influence.[8] Even before the end of the war, Attlee had pointed to the inescapable strategic consequences of Britain's geographical position in the world:

We are not a semi-detached country, free if we will to turn our backs on Europe and look towards the Atlantic, but a continental power with a valuable land frontier ... From our point of view, Norway, Denmark, Holland and France are necessary outposts of Britain ... Their defence is necessary to our defence, and without us they cannot defend themselves.[9]

The central issue was relations with France, and the story of the attempts in 1945-46 to create an Anglo-French alliance is one of failure. Most British historians relate the negative results of these negotiations to Anglo-French disagreements over the settlement in Syria and Lebanon, where the French suspected the British of intriguing against the French claims of control, and to the British objections to French ambitions in 1946 to deprive Germany of control of the Ruhr district. In other words, the British were willing to agree with France on a common European policy, but were rebuffed by French suspicions of British intentions in policy areas deemed to be vital to French interests.[10] The two sides agreed, however, on an agreement in March 1947 (The Dunkirk Treaty) to concert actions in the event of new German aggres-

---

[8] See Rasmus Mariager, *I tillid og varm sympati. Dansk-britiske forbindelser og USA under den tidlige kolde krig*, København: Museum Tusculanum Press 2006. Also s.a., 'Political Ambitions and Economic Realities: Anglo-Danish Relations and the US in the Early Cold War', in Jørgen Sevaldsen (ed.), *Britain and Denmark. Political, Economic and Cultural Relations in the 19th and 20th Centuries*, Copenhagen: Museum Tusculanum Press 2003, pp. 535-574.

[9] Attlee in 1945, quoted in N.P.Ludlow, 'Postwar Britain and Ideas of National Independence', in Dominik Geppert, ed., *The Postwar Challenge. Cultural, Social and Political Change in Western Europe, 1945-58*, Oxford University Press 2003, p. 267.

[10] See e.g. John W. Young, *Britain, France and the Unity of Europe, 1945-1951*, Leicester 1984 and Bullock, op. cit.

sion against any of the two countries. Later that year, however, the context changed. The USA returned to a more active role in international politics, exemplified by the Truman Doctrine and the Marshall Aid programme, and any hope that a division of Germany in Western and Eastern spheres of influence might be avoided had been abandoned. In that situation, exclusive Anglo-French combinations made little sense.

A 'Socialist Foreign Policy'?

Labour's election victory in 1945 had led to speculations about possible changes of direction in British foreign policy now that, for the first time in British history, the Labour Party had an absolute majority in the House of Commons. During the inter-war years, the main thrust of Labour's international policies had been towards internationalist and pacifist positions with an emphasis on disarmament and support of collective security.

The Labour Party in the House of Commons certainly included a left-wing fraction that urged a new, socialist foreign policy. It included about 50 MPs out of a Labour group of 393 and occasionally voiced its suspicions of US capitalism and called for support of the socialist forces in Continental countries. It also demanded a British policy that was independent of both the USA and the Soviet Union and backed nationalist movements in European colonies. The group was large and vociferous enough to disturb Bevin, but it was always defeated when votes were taken on issues of foreign policy at party conferences. By 1947, most of its members were backing Bevin's line in international affairs.[11]

In assessing Bevin's pragmatic and even traditional line in foreign policy it has to be remembered that the Labour party had been part of the coalition that ran Britain during the war. As Alan Bullock notes, Attlee and Bevin had had a big hand in formulating wartime policies. If you base your impressions of high politics during the war on what Churchill wrote in his wartime memoirs, as many have done, it would seem as if Churchill had personally arranged things with his partners

---

[11] Stefano Dejak, 'Labour and Europe during the Attlee Governments: the Image in the Mirror of R.W.C. Mackay's "Europe Group"', 1945-50', in Brian Brivati and Harriet Jones, *From Reconstruction to Integration: Britain and Europe since* 1945, Leicester University Press 1993, pp 47-57, analyses the internal discussions of the Labour Party on Europe and concludes that, in the end, ideas of 'socialist internationalism' had to take a back seat in the face of the 'deep scepticism, if not aversion, of the British people at large' to plans for European integration. (p. 56).

Roosevelt and Stalin. That was not the case – the important issues had been debated with the Labour leaders in advance, and charges in 1945 that Bevin was taking over Churchill's and Anthony Eden's Conservative polices were to that extent unfounded.[12] In 1945, Labour leaders like Attlee, Bevin and Herbert Morrison accepted that force might have to be used in international politics – a lesson obviously learned from the failures of the pre-war appeasement policy. The war had also changed their attitudes towards the Empire. British colonies were no longer seen as victims of evil imperialism but as powerful supports for Britain during the war and as a guarantee of her continued influence as a world power afterwards. So the change of government in 1945 did not radically change the outlook of the leaders responsible for the conduct of British foreign policy.

The Legacy of the Second World War

The interest among historians in British post-1945 attitudes towards the Continent is only one aspect of the continued fascination with the Legacy of the Second World War in Britain. A few of the most interesting historical controversies might be briefly outlined to serve as examples of the fundamental questions that are still being asked, in spite of the overall pride in Britain's achievements in the fight against Nazism.

Firstly, was it really worth it? To people who think that at the outbreak of the war Hitler would have been happy to leave Britain alone, it is tempting to argue that Britain should have kept out of the war. Thus, in 1975, the holocaust-denying ultra-right-wing author David Irving in his biography of Hitler wrote that since the German leader "originally had neither the intention nor the desire to harm Britain or destroy the empire, surely British readers at least must ask themselves: what, then, were we really fighting for?"[13] This theme came into public prominence in the 1990s after the publication of the neo-conservative and Eurosceptic historian John Charmley's biography *Churchill. The End of Glory*. Charmley again pointed to the disastrous results of the war for Britain. Churchill's main aim in life, he wrote, had been to preserve the British Empire and to fight Bolshevism. In 1945, a combination of Britain's relative economic and military weakness vis-à-vis the US and the Soviet Union meant that she was unable

---

[12] Bullock, op. cit., p. 65.
[13] David Irving: *Hitler's War and the War Path 1933-1945*, London: Focal Point 1975/1991), p. 21.

for long to maintain her Empire, the Soviets had extended their dominance into Central Europe, a Labour government was taking over in Britain herself, and Britain had become an appendix to the USA. Britain had fought valiantly and for a noble cause, but Charmley thinks that Britain's national interests would have been better served if Churchill had explored the possibility of a separate peace with Germany in 1940. If that could have been arranged, the British Empire might have had a longer lease of life and might have been able to steer her own course independently of the US and of the Continent.[14] Charmley's iconoclasm was widely condemned. Fellow historians were quick to point out that no responsible British leader could have trusted Hitler in 1940, that even if Britain was in a relatively weakened position in 1945, it came out of the war with her self-respect intact, and that in any case the British population was better served by being an American satellite than by living in the shadow of a victorious German Nazi Reich.[15]

A second version of the accusations against the British elite in 1945 of living in a world of illusions is the one which the military historian Corelli Barnett launched in 1986 in his book *The Audit of War: The Illusion and Reality of Britain as a Great Nation*.[16] Barnett's work was a contribution to the 'Decline of Britain' debate of the 1980s, and his diagnosis of Britain's economic problems of that time was that they were a result of the way in which politicians of the early 1940s grossly overestimated Britain's economic capabilities. They had been blind to the dependence of Britain on American technology and money during the war, and should have concentrated on improving British industrial competitiveness instead of dreaming of a 'New Jerusalem' and launching an expensive welfare state after 1945.

---

[14] John Charmley, *Churchill. The End of Glory*, London: Sceptre 1993, p. 649 and *passim*; s.a., *Churchill's Great Alliance*, London: Sceptre, 1995, p. 46. See also Jørgen Sevaldsen, 'Unødvendige og forgæves ofre? Storbritanniens deltagelse i Første og Anden Verdenskrig', in Carsten Due-Nielsen (ed.), *Historie og historiografi. Festskrift til Inga Floto*, København: Den Danske Historiske Forening 2002), p. 254-275, and s.a., 'Churchill, the Continuing Story', in *Nordic Journal of English Studies*, no. 1, 2005, vol. 4, p. 137-155.

[15] E.g. in Geoffrey Best, *Churchill. A Study in* Greatness, London: Hambledon and London 2001, p. 172.

[16] Corelli Barnett, *The Audit of War: The Illusion and Reality of Britain as a Great Nation*, London: Macmillan 1986. See also Jørgen Sevaldsen, 'Forfaldets fascination: "The decline of Britain" debatten', in *Historisk Tidsskrift*, vol. 88, 2, 1988, pp. 282-312.

Barnett's analysis clearly came from a Conservative political point of view, and his thesis has been dismissed by historians who doubt whether any government in 1945 could have neglected the deep longings of ordinary Britons for improvements in the social security systems. In fact, a third way of looking at the 'reality or illusions' debate has been suggested by historians who regret that conservative forces in Britain have hijacked the memory of the war. Thus, in *We can take it* (2004), Mark Conelly contrasts a 'Finest Hour' with a 'People's War' memory of the war. The first one has strengthened a conservative interpretation of British history by stressing Churchillian visions of standing alone against Continental tyranny, British military heroism and an exceptionalist view of British democracy. The 'People's War' version, in contrast, has been seen as unheroic and has been associated with socialism and unrealistic ambitions of the kind that Corelli Barnett denounced. Conelly partly blames the left wing in Britain for this and claims that non-conservative writers have leant over backwards in their attempts to distance themselves from celebratory accounts of British heroism during the war. The time has come, he concludes, to tell a story of Britain and the Second World War which allows people to feel pride in the British war effort without subscribing to an isolationist and conservative view of British destinies.[17]

European Unity? The Role of Winston Churchill

The debate about postwar British reactions to ideas of European unity immediately after the end of the war naturally revolves around these questions of which lessons the British had learnt from their war experiences. Winston Churchill himself has often been at the center of these discussions. His attitudes present a neat paradox. On the one hand he was the embodiment of the imperial 'Finest Hour' version of the British war. On the other hand, he quickly established himself as a leading proponent of European reconciliation and unity.

Churchill's main claim to fame in this respect is the speech he made in Zürich in September 1946 on the European situation. At that time, he was the leader of the opposition in Britain and spent a good deal of time travelling around the world to receive honours and speak on contemporary issues. Earlier in that year, in March 1946, he made his famous 'iron curtain' speech in Fulton, Missouri, on the need for Anglo-American co-operation in the face of Soviet totalitarian threats. In Zurich, he argued that the situation on the Continent was so serious that

---

[17] Mark Connelly, *We Can Take It!*, London: Longman 2004.

only a reconciliation between France and Germany could save European civilisation:

> *...there is a remedy which, if it were generally and spontaneously adopted, would as if by a miracle transform the whole scene, and would in a few years make all Europe, or the greater part of it, as free and as happy as Switzerland is today. What is this sovereign remedy? It is to re-create the European Family, or as much of it as we can, and provide it with freedom. We must build a kind of United States of Europe ... I am now going to say something that will astonish you. The first step in the re-creation of the European family must be a partnership between France and Germany. In this way only can France recover the moral leadership of Europe. There can be no revival of Europe without a spiritually great France and a spiritually great Germany. The structure of the United States of Europe, if well and truly built, will be such as to make the material strength of a single state less important. Small nations will count as much as large ones and gain their honour by their contribution to the common cause ... In all this urgent work, France and Germany must take the lead together. Great Britain, the British Commonwealth of Nations, mighty America, and I trust Soviet Russia – for then indeed all would be well – must be the friends and sponsors of the new Europe and must champion its right to live and shine.*[18]

At a time when the memory of the war was so recent and when the full extent of Nazi atrocities had just been demonstrated at the Nuremberg trials, a call for Franco-German reconciliation and partnership was indeed a brave and visionary action on the part of Churchill. What he wanted to do, no doubt, in his two important speeches in 1946 was to rally the democratic parts of Europe to co-operate in the face of the Soviet threat, while keeping an open door to the USA. The reception of his Zurich speech was, however, rather cool in many places. It was criticised by many for taking the division of Europe into a Western and a Communist bloc for granted, and by French politicians for talking about Germany as a unified nation at a time when some Frenchmen still hoped to see a decentralised Germany emerge from the war. In a Conservative Danish newspaper, a commentator concluded that Chur-

---

[18] Winston Churchill, speech in Zürich, 19 September 1946. David Cannadine (ed.), *The Speeches of Winston Churchill*, Penguin Books 1990, p. 310.

chill's concern about European unity was pure rhetoric and that the core of his message was a dream of Anglo-American dominance of European affairs.[19]

It was clear for all to see that in Zurich Churchill did not speak of Britain as a part of a United Europe, but as an outside sponsor of Continental integration. Nevertheless, he went on to make other speeches that seemed to include Britain in the European family and even accepted a development towards supra-national institutions, but these were again contradicted by statements that linked Britain to the Empire and to the idea of national sovereignty.[20] The one single utterance from him that best sums up the ambivalence of his views on Britain's relationship with Europe is, perhaps, an article he wrote way back in 1930. Here, he explained to an American audience his support for the European federal ideas of Count Coudenhove-Kalergi, but then added:

> ... *The attitude of Great Britain towards European unification or 'federal links' would, in the first instance, be determined by her dominant conception of a united British Empire. Every step that tends to make Europe more prosperous and more peaceful is conducive to British interests ... We are bound to further every honest and practical step which the nations of Europe may make to reduce the barriers which divide them and to nourish their common interests and their common welfare ... We see nothing but good and hope in a richer, freer, more contented European commonalty. But we have our own dream and our own task. We are with Europe, but not of it. We are linked, but not comprised. We are interested and associated, but not absorbed.* [21]

Nevertheless, Churchill went on to put himself at the head of a United Europe movement and to play an important role in the development of

---

[19] 'Hans Tale om et forenet Europa, selvstændigt og selvhjulpen i Samvirken med udenforstaaende Verdensmagter, [er] kun en retorisk Blomst ... Kernen i hans Forkyndelse er et England, sluttet op til USA og et USA med den økonomiske og imperiale Struktur, det har i 1946, et, der siger vor Verdensdels små og store Magter Besked ...' *Berlingske Aftenavis* 24. September 1946. See also Jørgen Sevaldsen, *Churchill, Statsmand og Myte*, København: Aschehoug 2004, p. 330 ff; and Max Beloff, 'Churchill and Europe', in Robert Blake and Wm. Robert Louis (eds.), *Churchill*, Oxford University Press 1993, pp. 443-455.

[20] See Sevaldsen 2004, p. 333 ff.

[21] Winston S. Churchill, 'The United States of Europe', *Saturday Evening Post*, 15 February 1930. Printed in Michael Wolff, ed. *The Collected Essays of Sir Winston Churchill*, Library of Imperial History 1976, vol. II, p. 184.

European institutions in the late 1940s. Thus, he hosted the Hague Conference in 1948 that led to the establishment of the Council of Europe in 1949. In that sense, he was one of the fathers of Europe. In Britain, the contradictory nature of his statements on Britain's relations with her Continental partners has led to a situation where both Europhiles and Eurosceptics can find quotes from him in support of their positions. As a contemporary illustration of his position as an icon of supporters of the EU in Britain, the following letter to the BBC from 2002 on the subject of Britain and the Euro may be quoted:

Having just returned from two weeks in France I can honestly say that British resistance to the Euro is indicative of a wider malaise affecting this country. We whine and moan about the continent and about accepting the Euro, yet we lap up continental foods, sports, sun and culture like thirsty nomads; instead of being a strong leader in Euro we are dogmatic and belligerent, unwilling to adapt because of a perceived superiority (the true reason for our resistance), as well as still fighting WWII. My grandfather, a 78 year old veteran of the campaign, has no problems with concepts surrounding the Euro, neither did Winston Churchill (1946). As a Welshman, I find it laughable that people think that I would be willing to sacrifice my culture and heritage. Jon Kingsbury, United Kingdom, EU.[22]

When, however, Churchill's European ambitions came to the test in his second period as Prime Minister from 1951 to 1955, it became clear that he was as sceptical towards supra-national institutions in Europe as his Labour predecessors had been. And this is what has made many Europhile historians conclude that on balance, Churchill's efforts may have been more harmful to Britain's long-time interests than beneficial. Thus a recent biographer, the otherwise Churchill-friendly historian John Ramsden concludes that

What remains most striking, however, after this lengthy reiteration of the extremely high regard with which both Churchill and Britain itself were held across Europe after 1945, is, as Professor M.R.D. Foot has put it, the recklessness with which such a national asset was wasted by British governments over the next two

---

[22] BBC Talking Point: What do you think of the Euro? 10 January 2002. http//news.bbc.co.uk/1/hi/talking_point/1737171.stm

decades. Whatever role Britain might have sought to play after 1945, Churchill had ensured that the ball was at our feet, though somehow neither he nor his successors were ever able to run with it. This was a failure of foreign policy that could well come to weigh heavily in the historical scales of judgement.[23]

Missing the European Bus?

Ramsden's complaint is an echo of similar charges against British decision-makers made by politicians and historians disappointed by Britain's lukewarm attitudes towards the early attempts to interest her in further European integration. A classic example is the comments made in 1960 by the Conservative politician Anthony Nutting in his book *Europe Will Not Wait*. Nutting, too, makes the point that Britain could have had the leadership of Europe if she had been interested:

> ... If we had offered our hand it would have been grasped without question or condition. But Great Britain was ruled then by men whose political philosophy was as magnificently limited as the London bus conductor who observed after the fall of France in 1940, 'Well, thank God we're playing the final on the home ground' ... for all their internationalist preaching of the past, the Labour party when they took office could scarcely have been more insular and nationalist, even blimpish, in their European policy ... As had happened before in 1929, when Ramsay Macdonald's government declined to support the initiative of Aristide Briand for a European League of Nations, the Labour government, when put to the test, preferred insularity to internationalism.[24]

Most writers now dismiss this as an inadequate description of Britain's policies immediately after the end of the war. Prominent experts in Britain's relations with Western Europe such as N. Piers Ludlow and Alan S. Milward have attacked what they term the 'price of victory' thesis, i.e. that Britain kept aloof from the Continent because she did not, like France, Italy and Germany experience defeat and therefore – mistakenly – believed that there was no reason why she should give up the belief in a purely national framework for economic and diplomatic

---

[23] John Ramsden, *Man of the Century. Winston Churchill and his Legend since 1945*, London: HarperCollins 2002), p. 321.

[24] Quoted in Geoffrey Warner, 'The Labour Governments and the Unity of Western Europe, 1945-51', in Ritchie Ovendale, *The Foreign Policy of the British Labour Governments, 1945-1951*, Leicester University Press 1984, p. 61.

decisions. Firstly, they refer to the positive initiatives that Bevin took in those years e.g. vis-à-vis France as proof that British policy makers were, in fact, interested in promoting European co-operation at this time. Secondly, they ask whether Attlee's and Bevin's views of Britain's short-term and long-term advantages were not, in fact, quite sound in the circumstances of 1945. The truth, according to Milward, is that Britain possessed many advantages after the war which it was only natural that her government tried to exploit. Western Europe, however, did not offer much scope for British successes. Apart from Germany, most of the countries were not desperately poor and experienced a reasonably rapid economic growth. They did not really need Britain. "It is not true", Milward asserts, "that the UK had a fund of goodwill in Europe arising from its wartime role on which it could have traded to lead Europe in support of shared common interests. Europe was not asking to be led. It had not so many shared common interests with Britain."[25] In this analysis, Britain's advantages were much more usable outside Europe. Among them were the system of tariff preferences with the Commonwealth countries, London's traditions as an international capital market, Britain's strategic usefulness to the USA as a naval and air base, and the country's large armed forces. The latter were criticised as excessive, but they were seen by British leaders as bargaining counters that the UK could use to attain its objectives. It would, it was felt, have been foolish to give them away for nothing. This is not to say that politicians and officials did not realise that these inherited advantages were temporary and that something longer lasting should be sought, or that they doubted that at some point Europe would return to its position as major market for Britain. Europe was never dismissed as a long-term partner. But normalisation had, it turned out, to wait on the increasing delays and frustrations imposed by economic difficulties in Britain in the late 1940s. So Milward thinks that the 'One World' rather than 'European' strategy chosen in 1945 was sensible and may be seen as a rational way of adjusting to the postwar world. He admits that the strategy did not prove very successful, but failure was not necessarily because of British choices but because of the economic policies pursued by others, e.g. the failure by the USA to reduce tariffs.

Ludlow agrees with Milward that the emphasis on Commonwealth links in 1945 was natural and understandable, and also stresses that

---

[25] Alan S. Milward, *The Rise and Fall of a National Strategy 1945-1963*, London: Cass 2002, p. 12. See also N. Piers Ludlow, 'Paying the Price of Victory? Postwar Britain and the Ideas of National Independence', in Geppert, op. cit., pp 259-271.

Bevin's extensive involvement in Western European institutions and politics in 1945-49 gives a lie to accusations that Britain was anti-European in this period. He admits, however, that the Second World War experience had tended to confirm British feelings of superiority vis-à-vis the Continent and thus helped to create a psychological barrier towards involving the country too deeply in supra-national projects:

> ...*the shadow of the Second World War has influenced and continues to influence the British debate about Europe and has helped to keep alive a series of national myths and self-images which ought, more rationally, to have been jettisoned long ago.*[26]

Few British historians would, in other words, deny that at the psychological level, the Second World War tended to confirm Churchillian feelings of Britain being 'with Europe, but not of it'. At the same time, a robust attempt is now being made to defend the British politicians at the time against accusations that they alone were to blame for the lack of quick progress for European political and economic co-operation in the immediate postwar years. As indicated, much of the work done on early British responses to the European postwar challenges confirms that, in retrospect, it is extremely important to separate judgements on the 1945-46 period from analyses of British policies and attitudes in the years after 1947.

---

[26] Ludlow, op. cit., p. 272.

CHAPTER 4

IN AND OUT OF EUROPE
Spain 1945

Carsten Humlebæk

Spain was in a particularly delicate situation in 1939 at the outbreak of the Second World War, which began only five months after the so-called "national" troops under the leadership of general Francisco Franco had won the Spanish Civil War. Spain was destroyed by its fraternal war, not only physically and economically, but also in terms of its social fabric. Despite having controlled large parts of the territory for almost the entire length of the Civil War, by mid-1939 the new regime was only just in the process of consolidating itself and gaining control of the situation.

The recent history of Spain was evidence of a malfunctioning democracy and national disruption, as opposed to the consolidation of a common national project. Since 1875 an increasingly faulty constitutional monarchy had governed Spain. It was eventually overthrown in 1923 with the military coup of general Miguel Primo de Rivera. The following period of military dictatorship lasted for eight years until it was itself overthrown by popular discontent in 1930-1931, which resulted in the Second Republic. Despite the high hopes nurtured by a large portion of the Spanish population, the republican regime polarised every bit of political, social and religious life. After only five years of democratic republican regime the Civil War broke out in 1936.

The relationship with the rest of Europe was of a rather complex nature. The Spanish monarchy, after having participated in all major European wars from 1516 to 1808, did not take part in any armed European conflict from 1808 onwards and retained its neutrality during the First World War.[1] And although the Axis Powers as well as the Soviet Union had been directly involved in the Spanish Civil War, the Western victors of the Second World War had done their best to stay out of the Spanish Civil War, precisely due to the complicated international situation in the last half of the 1930's. Suffice to say that for Spain there could be no return to normality in 1945, since the relationship with the rest of Europe in any case had to be completely reconstructed. Neither could there be a real 'new beginning' in any positive sense due to the Franco regime's former relationship with Mussolini's Italy and Hitler's Germany and the dictatorial and at least partially Fascist character of the regime that was at odds with the dominant ideas of the victorious Western Allies.

The character, and ideological leanings, of the Franco regime have been the object of many academic studies.[2] To describe it as Fascist and authoritarian or totalitarian inevitably constitutes an oversimplification, unless a detailed account of its evolution over time is included. The regime stayed in power for a prolonged period of time in a very changeable international context and therefore unavoidably underwent important changes due to external as well as internal circumstances. To understand the dynamics of the Francoist period, however, it is important to grasp one fundamental fact: the Franco regime responded primarily to one goal, namely to keep Franco in power for as long as he wanted it. All other political, ideological and religious concerns would ultimately be secondary to this primary goal. Franco's remark to one of his leading generals is famous: "I shall not make the same mistake as Primo de Rivera. There will be no resignation: from here only to the cemetery".[3] Franco emerged from the Civil War with powers that no other ruler had ever had in Spain. He was very careful not to repeat the errors of the former regimes and very carefully adjusted his foreign as well as domestic policy according to what he felt to be the necessities of the moment. This was done, for example, through censorship, through adjusting the external image of the regime

---

[1] José Álvarez Junco, 'La nación en duda', in Juan Pan-Montojo (ed.), *Más se perdió Cuba : Espana, 1898 y la crisis de fin de siglo*, Madrid: Alianza 1998, p. 443.

[2] A good and concise presentation of this historiographical discussion can be found in Manuel Pérez Ledesma, 'Una dictadura "por la gracia de dios"', *Historia Social*, No. 20, 1994, pp. 173-193.

[3] The Primo de Rivera referred to in the quotation is, of course, Miguel Primo de Rivera, author of the military dictatorship from 1923 to 1930. Quoted in Stanley G. Payne: *The Franco Regime 1936-1975*, Madison: The University of Wisconsin Press 1987, p. 349.

and – perhaps most importantly – by changing the composition of his successive governments.

During the increasingly difficult international period before the outbreak of the Second World War, Franco coined a term to describe the foreign policy of his regime: "hábil prudencia", which can be translated as "adroit prudence".[4] Although pro-German by instinct and affinity, this political caution made Franco avoid what would have been the logical consequences – in foreign as well as domestic politics – of his pro-German beliefs. He thus avoided both direct involvement in the war, at least on the western fronts, as well as the greater pursuit of Fascist doctrines and practices. Spain did participate with a corps of volunteers, the Blue Division, in Hitler's war against the Soviet Union, but the size of the operation was carefully adjusted so as not to provoke any declarations of war. The result of Franco's prudence was a policy characterised by opportunism and diplomatic zig-zagging, which also earned Franco the enmity of both the Western Allies as well as Nazi Germany.[5]

The initially uncertain prospects for Germany's success dictated a policy of "neutrality", already declared on the 4th of September 1939. After these initial doubts Franco began to believe that Germany would win the war and therefore slowly adopted a more openly pro-German alignment emphasising the Fascist/Falangist elements of the regime. Though definitely tempted, Franco prudently resisted Hitler's pressure to make Spain participate directly in the war, but from the 12th of June 1940 the official policy was termed "non-belligerence". His sympathies had been with Germany since the very beginning, but only now had the official foreign policy of "hábil prudencia" acquired a clear leaning towards the Axis powers.[6]

In late 1942 the war moved closer to Spain. On the one hand, there was the Operation Torch of the Allied landing in Northwest Africa and, on the other hand, Germany occupied the whole of France up to the Spanish border. Spain was caught between two fires. This recommended a new kind of caution aimed at resisting any kind of foreign occupation – both German and Allied – as well as maintaining at least some goodwill from both sides. In practice this was done, firstly, by a

---

[4] Payne, op.cit., p. 255.
[5] Raymond Carr, *Spain 1808-1975,* Oxford: Clarendon Press 1982, p. 710, and Payne, op.cit., p. 266.
[6] Christian Leitz, 'Nazi Germany and Francoist Spain, 1936 – 1945', in Sebastian Balfour & Paul Preston (eds.), *Spain and the Great Powers in the Twentieth Century,* London: Routledge 1999, pp. 136-137.

partial mobilisation of the army in order to dissuade Hitler from entering Spain, secondly, by not interfering with the operation of the Allies in Northern Africa and their passage through the Strait of Gibraltar and, thirdly, by keeping up deliveries of raw materials to both sides, principally iron ore to Britain and wolfram to Germany. The image conscious Franco began to tone down the Fascist components of the regime; in fact he made his last openly Fascist remarks in late 1942. Still hoping for a German victory, Franco surely began to entertain the possibility of an Allied victory as well, which meant a drive towards Western values and some sort of 'democratisation' of the regime. This implied redefining the meaning of totalitarian, and efforts were thus made to distinguish the Franco regime as representing a particular Spanish brand of Catholic authoritarianism, as distinct from the central European authoritarian regimes. Furthermore the regime was given a democratic varnish as a corporative parliament was opened in March 1943 just after Hitler's Stalingrad defeat, which instilled further doubts about German victory. Conscious of the difficulty that the relationship to Germany and Italy would constitute should the Allies win the war, Franco tried to scoop out an independent position for his regime by insisting on its anti-Communism. The regime, for example, promoted a diplomatic peace initiative among the other neutral countries between January and February 1943 to help mediate a peace between Germany and the Allies and join forces against bolchevism. In his effort to split East and West Franco would from then on speak of the three wars: the German vs. Allied conflict in which Spain was neutral, the German vs. Soviet Union conflict in which Spain was pro-German, and the Allied vs. Japan conflict in which Spain was pro-Allied. On October 1, 1943, the official policy was altered from "non-belligerence" to "vigilant neutrality" and the Blue Division was called back.

It was only in mid-1944 that Franco gave up his hopes that Germany would win the war and so began a more genuine alignment with the Allies. The tension over the wolfram exports to Germany caused a crisis in the relationship with the Allied powers, but the conflict was settled with an agreement in May 1944. In August of the same year the Spanish press was ordered to be more neutral in its coverage of the war. With regards to the external image of the regime, the main emphasis was now put on the Catholic character of the regime, understating somewhat its anti-Communism. This new alignment with the Western powers among the Allies would remain in place also after the end of the Second World War.

As both sides considered Spain to be of only secondary strategic importance, Spain was neither drawn into the war nor suffered any invasion. As the war developed, both Nazi-Germany and the Western Allies had relatively similar goals with respect to Spain: on the one hand to impede the capture of the peninsula's strategic position and resources by the other side and, on the other, to keep Franco-led Spain out of the war, trying to keep him as favourably inclined towards them as possible. The major failure of the Francoist regime was not to have returned to neutrality in 1942 upon American entry into the war, when it would have cost less and counted most. The real shift in 1944 came too late. On the other hand, the war years were fundamental for the consolidation of Franco's regime. The successive reorganisations of governments and the partial re-elaborations of regime image were not only meant to position Spain favourably in the international context; they also served to solidify his own leadership.[7]

The Allied victory in the Second World War placed Spain in an outsider position in postwar Western Europe. Franco and his regime constituted an anomaly in the eyes of the winning coalition, which judged Spain not only by its opportunistic policy during the war but also – and more importantly – by the way it came to power through the assistance of the Axis powers during the Civil War. Spain was excluded from the construction of the new international society and pressure was exercised to favour the departure of general Franco and the substitution of him by a democratic system of some sort. If Spain in 1939 at the end of the Civil War had entered a postwar period characterised by extreme hardship and difficult recovery, in 1945 a second postwar period – or the prolongation of the first – began, which was to last until well into the 1950's.

The international acceptance of Spain seemed conditioned on internal political change. At the San Francisco Conference in June 1945 of what was to become the United Nations, a motion was approved on the initiative of Mexico that banned Spanish membership of the new organisation due to Italy's and Germany's help during the Civil War. The motion, however, also contained a passage inspired by the British stating that the Allies would not intervene directly in Spanish affairs. Shortly afterwards, at the Potsdam Conference in early August 1945, the Allies took up the discussion of the policy towards Spain on which they did not agree. Russia and France favoured an economic and diplomatic blockade of Spain, whereas Britain was sharply opposed to

---

[7] Payne, op.cit., pp. 340-342; Carr, op.cit., pp. 713-715.

this idea because it would mean intervening in Spain's internal affairs and so violating the San Francisco Charter. Furthermore, in London, it was believed that a blockade would only reinforce Franco's position. The United States maintained an intermediate position but ended up accepting the British argument. After lengthy discussions at Potsdam a similar communiqué to that of San Francisco was approved.[8]

For Franco the result was a victory since it proved the validity of what had been his policy since 1943-44, namely to insist on the regime's anti-Communism and wait for the conflict between the capitalist West and Communist Soviet Union to detonate. Franco's right hand and later successor as Head of Government, Luis Carrero Blanco, in late August 1945 articulated the victorious policy of the dictatorship like this:

> *If you stop to think about it for a moment, it must be recognised that in Potsdam we had been defended energetically by Truman and by Churchill (...) They defended us for their **own interests** (...) [W]hen the last shot was fired in the Pacific, a diplomatic war broke out between the Anglo-Saxons and Russia (...) Out of this basic **cold interest**, the Anglo-Saxons will not only not support, but will oppose everything they can which might lead to a situation of Soviet hegemony on the Iberian Peninsula. Their interests here are based on order and anti-Communism, but they would prefer to achieve this with a regime other than the existing one (...) Pressure from the Anglo-Saxons for a change in Spanish politics which would interrupt the normal evolution of the existing regime will ease off the more tangible our **order**, **unity** and **impassivity** become in the face of orders, threats and impertinences. The only formula left to us is: **order, unity and to endure**.* [Emphasis in original].[9]

The quotation demonstrates just how clearly the international position of Spain in the immediate postwar period was perceived by the regime

---

[8] Pedro Martínez Lillo, 'La política exterior de España en el marco de la Guerra Fría: del aislamiento limitado a la integración parcial en la sociedad international, 1945-1953', in Javier Tusell, Juan Avilés & Rosa Pardo, *La política exterior de España en el siglo XX*, Madrid: Biblioteca Nueva 2000, pp. 330-331. See also Florentino Portero, 'Spain, Britain and the Cold War', in Balfour & Preston (eds.), op.cit., pp. 215-216, and Payne, op.cit. p. 339.

[9] The admission has been described by José Luis Messia, *Por palabra de honor: la entrada de España en el Consejo de Europa*, Madrid: Parteluz 1995. Messia was the Spanish observer at the Council of Europe. Quoted in Portero, op.cit., p. 216.

itself. Franco had been right to believe that relations with the Soviet Union would be a key element in the definition of Spain's new role. Despite the evident reluctance to intervene directly in Spanish affairs, the immediate postwar years nevertheless was a period when the survival of the Franco regime, isolated in an increasingly hostile Europe, seemed to be in doubt. The possibility that the victorious Allies would act in order to restore democracy thus made the opposition against Franco – republicans, left wing political parties as well as Basques and Catalans – hope that their day had come.

Time would eventually show that these hopes were in vain. From 1945 to 1947 the Basque republican government-in-exile tried to exert international pressure on the Allies in order to drag them into opposition against the dictatorship but, overall, the impact of these efforts was limited. In 1945 a Basque Consultative Council was set up to co-ordinate clandestine activity in the Basque Country, but the actions and the networks were easily uncovered and severely repressed by Spanish police forces. In 1951, as the Franco regime was slowly coming in from the cold, the Western powers withdrew support from the Basque government-in-exile, isolating the Basque nationalists who generally lost their hopes. The Western democracies thus did not succeed in isolating the Franco regime, which led the Basques to conclude that they could not depend on help outside of Spain. This is one of the most important explanations of the birth of ETA less than ten years later.[10] In addition, in Catalonia many people hoped that the Allied victory in the Second World War would help bring down the Franco regime that had initiated a harsh repression of Catalan language and culture immediately after the fall of Catalonia during the last phases of the Civil War. When it became clear around 1946-1947 that the Western powers did not plan to intervene in Spain in favour of a rapid reestablishment of democracy in Spain, the Catalan intelligentsia suffered a disillusionment not unlike their Basque equals. This conjuncture of repression and disillusion produced a real threat of a violent turn for Catalan nationalism, in the way in which it later happened in the Basque country. But in the end, the most radical Catalanists found a way of expressing their anxieties through the cultural nationalism that had developed in Catalonia since the mid-nineteenth century.[11]

The Spanish republican party leaders were in exile where they carried on the internal feuds of the Civil War. The Socialist Party strug-

---

[10] Daniele Conversi, *The Basques, the Catalans and Spain. Alternative Routes to Nationalist Mobilisation,* London: Hurst & Company 1997, pp. 80-83.
[11] Conversi, op.cit., pp. 109-117.

gled with the Communists to control exile funds and organisation, and the end of the world war did not alleviate these internal divisions. The socialists insisted that if the Republic was to be restored it must create a credible government out of the warring factions and exclude the Communists who would never be acceptable to the West. This new republican government-in-exile came into existence in September 1945. In this project there was no idea of a struggle in Spain; all hopes were focused on an overthrow of the Franco regime with the active help of the Allies. These hopes were disappointed.[12] If these groups never constituted any real threat to the regime, the monarchists were much more dangerous to Franco since their opposition came from within the regime. They had fought alongside Franco in the Civil War in order to bring an end to the republican regime and reestablish the monarchy. On various occasions monarchists from within the regime – e.g. army officers – had urged Franco to step down and reinstate the monarchy. Franco solved this problem with a two-fold tactic: by restating that Spain was a monarchy, but without ever making any clear promises as to who would eventually be King nor when. Franco maintained contacts with the legitimate pretender, Don Juan, but without ever making any statement in public. Franco never intended to pass the throne on to him, but wanted to avoid turning him against the regime out of concern for the monarchist supporters of the regime.[13]

Despite the reassurances that the Allies would not interfere directly in Spain, the Allied victory in 1945 convinced Franco of the need to reform the regime, if only on the surface, in order to survive in social democratic Western Europe. He therefore began to elaborate a series of so-called Fundamental Laws. The first of these to be passed was the *Fuero de los Españoles* from July 1945. It was a kind of Charter of Rights and described Spain as an organic democracy. The description emphasised the Catholic character of the regime and clearly understated the Falangist elements. Simultaneously, Franco carried through a change of his government along similar lines. The Catholics were thus allotted a more prominent place and the Falangists were relegated to a secondary position. In fact, Franco had hoped for a concordat with the Vatican soon after the end of the Civil War. But the experience of fraternisation with Fascist Italy and Hitler-Germany made the Vatican decline such a move. Nevertheless, the 1940's in Spain represented a period of revival of all aspects of religious life and endowment of pub-

---

[12] Javier Tusell, *Historia de España en el siglo XX. III. La Dictadura de Franco*, Madrid: Grupo Santillana 1998, pp. 183-197.
[13] Tusell, op.cit., pp. 202-209; Payne, op.cit., pp. 325-332.

lic life with sacred elements.[14] The moves towards organic democracy and the changed internal balance of the regime in favour of the Catholics did not convince the rest of Europe, wherein opinion was shifting towards the left wing that maintained a very critical opinion of Franco's Spain. France temporarily closed the border with Spain in the summer of 1945 and again in March 1946 indefinitely. The United Nations continued its pressure on Spain and in December 1946 a resolution urged all member states to close down all diplomatic relations with Spain on demanding a democratisation of the country.[15] In general terms the regime responded to the international criticism and isolation with ostracism. Franco portrayed this campaign as being anti-Spanish and the result of a Communist-Masonic conspiracy against Spain; the effect was that the Spaniards rallied in support of the regime. It thus strengthened the regime instead of weakening it, exactly as the British had foreseen at the San Francisco and Potsdam discussions. The main strategy chosen by the regime to achieve legitimacy during the period of ostracism was to further accentuate the Catholic identity as well as intensify the function of monarchism in the description of the regime.[16]

So far – during his first nine years – Franco had stayed in power by keeping everything temporary and by not choosing sides during the war, which was related mainly to the European context. In the case of Axis victory a perpetual dictatorship would have been a very likely outcome, but Franco had kept the possibility of an authoritarian monarchy open in the event of an Allied victory. But slowly impressions were shifting and other problems became more important, in particular the relationship with the Soviet Union and Communism. The definitive turn came with the Truman doctrine which was made public on March 12, 1947. It presented a vision of a polarised world for and against Communism, which opened new perspectives for a re-legitimisation of Spain.

Franco used this occasion to formulate an authoritarian monarchy on his own terms by passing the so-called Succession Law on March 27, 1947, only a fortnight after the Truman doctrine. Its first article read: "Spain, as a political unit, is a Catholic, social, and representative state which, in keeping with her tradition, declares herself constituted into a kingdom." In the second article the kind of kingdom was specified: "The Head of State is the caudillo of Spain and of the Crusade, Gener-

---

[14] Payne, op.cit., pp. 349-369.
[15] Tusell, op.cit., pp. 213-215.
[16] Portero, op.cit., pp. 218-222.

alissimo of the Armed Forces, Don Francisco Franco Bahamonde". According to the law, Spain was a monarchy under Franco's regency; Franco was the sovereign constitutional organ of the State with the right to designate the future king of Spain. The law was designed to legitimise Franco as supreme head of state who, in practice, could not be relieved of his duty. To legitimise the law and the institutional set-up created by it, the law was then passed by a referendum on the issue with 92 % in favour of the law out of a turnout of 88%.[17]

By then, in 1947, it was becoming more and more apparent that international pressure on the regime as well as internal insurgency against it was waning. The repeated discussions of Spain in international fora and the United Nations' resolution against the country were a product of an attempt to maintain the Second World War alliance against Fascism. But with Truman's declaration of the Cold War, the situation changed radically, which paved the way out of isolation for Spain as Franco had foreseen already during the war. A Soviet-inspired United Nations initiative against Spain in November 1947 failed. France opened the frontier again in February 1948, and in May, Spain negotiated commercial agreements with France and Britain. Across the Atlantic, the Spanish lobby in the United States was successful in altering US policy towards Spain during 1949-1950. Political – principally anti-Communist – and geo-strategic considerations were the key factors. Loans were given to Spain and in November 1950 the 1946 United Nations resolution was repealed and the most severe isolation was ended.[18]

If Franco had been wrong about the possibility of a German victory and had not chosen the optimal moment to revert to neutrality, he was right about the fact that the anti-Communist stance of the regime was to be a key element in the definition of Spain's new role in the post-1945 international context. All the regime had to do was to resist the external pressures, explain that the monarchy was on its way and wait for the international context to change, as Carrero Blanco had described it.

So if Spain was mostly 'out' of Europe in 1945, the Cold War facilitated its way back, if not into Europe, then into the waiting room of Europe; not as a full and equal member of democratic Western Europe, but as a tolerated part of the political continent. And, what was most

---

[17] Payne, op.cit., pp. 371-375 (quotations on p. 372). See also Tusell, op.cit., pp. 172-174.
[18] Martínez Lillo, op.cit., pp. 335-340. See also Portero, op.cit., pp. 224-226; Tusell, op.cit., pp. 216-226 and Payne, op.cit., pp. 381-383.

important for Franco himself, with a tacit acceptance of Franco as almighty head of state in Spain.

The Allies had abstained from intervening directly in Spain during the aftermath of the Second World War, and as Francoist Spain was gradually accepted by its European neighbours, it began to interact more and more intensely with the rest of Europe. Towards the end of the dictatorship in the 1970s, both factors helped pave the way for Spain's consensual transition to democracy and its full re-entry into Europe.

CHAPTER 5

ALL ROADS LEAD TO ROME
Fascism and Anti-Fascism in Postwar Italy

Morten Heiberg

In 1932, the Italian dictator Benito Mussolini put forward his revolutionary ideas in a speech addressed to a fanatic crowd in Milan. In his talk, he not only presented his ideas for a new, Fascist Europe, he also tried to persuade the citizens of Milan that the future of Fascism was the eternal city of Rome. This was indeed a remarkable statement. A *Romagnolo* from the small town of Predappio, Mussolini had spent most of his youth in Milan, and Fascism itself was originally a North Italian phenomenon.

In his Milan speech, he emphasised that "the 20th century is going to be the century of Fascism, it is going to be the century of Italian power; it is going to be the century in which Italy returns for the third time to become the leader of human civilisation. In ten years, one might say without acting as a prophet that Europe will be changed…In ten years Europe will be Fascist or *Fascistised*."[1] One of the ways to achieve this goal was to support movements or political parties outside Italy, which would overthrow the existing order and create a Fascist regime loyal to 'the doctrine and wisdom of Rome'. The same year, Mussolini supported a failed military coup in Spain, and soon other na-

---

[1] Benito Mussolini, speech in Milan, 25 October 1932. Cf. Benito Mussolini, *Opera Omnia*, Florence: La Fenice 1958, vol. XXV, p. 147; Morten Heiberg, 'Mussolini, Franco and the Spanish Civil War', in Gert Sørensen & Robert Mallet (eds.), *International Fascism 1919-1945*, London: Frank Cass 2002, pp. 61-62.

tions, carefully selected because of their presumed military weakness, received an even rougher treatment.[2]

To Europe's good fortune, the continent was able to resist Mussolini's *Fascismo d'esportazione*. Ten years after Mussolini's speech, the situation was reversed: the Allied forces stood at the Italian gate, and from 1943, Mussolini's Social Republic in North Italy, backed by German Nazi occupation forces, fought a desperate death struggle against the Reign in the South, the coalition of Communist, socialist, liberal and Christian-democratic resistance and, not least, the Allied Forces. In April 1945, Mussolini was shot and his mutilated body was exposed hanging up-side down on a market square in Milan, the very city from where, in 1932, he had demonstrated his own will power and prophesised the final triumph of Fascism in Europe. Milan had indeed marked both the beginning and the end of Mussolini's flirtation with the third imperial Rome.

The fall of Fascism resulted in a new era for Italy and certainly also for Europe as a whole. It paved the way for a new Italian Republic with a democratic constitution based on distinct anti-Fascist principles. Less than a decade after the formation of the Republic, in 1957, the Treaty of the European Community was signed in Rome. For France, Germany, Luxembourg, Belgium, the Netherlands, and Italy the treaty was an important step towards European co-operation, unity and stability. The signing parties made the historical agreement to pool "their resources to preserve and strengthen peace and liberty, and calling upon the other peoples of Europe who share their ideal to join in their efforts".[3] The choice of Rome for the signing of the treaty was hardly a coincidence. For the signing parties, and for the fathers of the new Italian Republic in particular, it symbolised the final break-away from the previous Fascist experience and imperialism, which had led to an unprecedented disaster in Italian history. For now on, the city of Rome should no longer be associated with the aggressive nationalism of the past, but only with parliamentary democracy, international co-operation, and peace.

Still, does that mean that with the rise of a new Republic committed to European collaboration Fascism had finally been defeated, and that democracy and internationalism had now become the dominant ideologies in Italian society? For sure, if one looks at the official symbols,

---

[2] Cf. Lucio Ceva, 'The Strategy of Fascist Italy, A Premise', in Gert Sørensen & Robert Mallet (eds.), *International Fascism 1919-1945*, London: Frank Cass 2002, pp. 41-54.
[3] *Treaty Establishing the European Community*, Rome, 25 March 1957, Preamble.

buildings and monuments employed by the new regime, one still senses the presence of a strange legacy of the past. Nowhere are the signs of continuity and rupture between the past Fascist regime and the postwar Republic more visible than in the architecture of Rome. After the Allied occupation, the impressive EUR area was fenced in. The EUR is an unfinished Fascist replica of the ancient Rome, built by Mussolini for a 1942 World Exhibition. The immediate intention of the new government was to tear it down as yet another sign of rupture with the former regime. However, as government bureaucracy began to expand, the area was put back into use, and in this way important masterpieces of modern Italian architecture were saved for posterity. Even more significant is the treatment of the area around *Foro Mussolini*, now known as the *Foro Italico*. The square was originally inaugurated to celebrate the first anniversary of the proclamation of the Italian Empire in 1937. In front of a rectangular *piazza* one can still observe today an obelisk with the inscription 'Mussolini DUX'. Two rows of marble stones on the side of the piazza recall important events in the history of Fascism: the First World War, the foundation of the regime, the new cities in the Pontine Marshes, and the war in Ethiopia. On the eighteenth stone appears suddenly the words: ("Fine del regime Fascista") or "end of the Fascist regime". The following inscriptions commemorate the end of the Italian monarchy and the republican constitution of 1948.[4] The fact that the leaders of the new Republic did not demolish the monument, but found it sufficient to adjust its meaning simply by adding a new inscription is indeed noteworthy and perhaps even symbolic. In the 1950s, much in the same way, the Christian Democrats built their own economic power centres within the new Republic by largely exploiting the Fascist edifice, understood as the efficient system for state-intervention and control over the economy created by the former regime.

Since 1945, Italy's road from Fascist dictatorship and a bloody civil war towards an anti-Fascist and distinctly democratic society has been long and winding and with several setbacks along the way. As in other European countries, the logic of the Cold War impeded a proper showdown with some of the fiercest and most repressive Fascist elements within the state administration. We need only to think of the element within the army and the police, who could have been purged, but instead were employed in clandestine battles against the Communists,

---

[4] Steen Bo Frandsen, 'The war that we prefer: The Reclamation of the Pontine Marshes and Fascist Expansionism', in Gert Sørensen & Robert Mallet (eds.), *International Fascism 1919-1945*, London: Frank Cass 2002, p. 81.

who soon established themselves as Italy's second largest political grouping. In 1960, a calculation revealed that only two out of 64 prefects (the central government's representative in the Italian provinces) had not been functionaries under Fascism.[5] Between 1945 and 1970 more than five thousand Italians were wounded and 156 killed by the *carabinieri* or by the police during manifestations for fundamental rights. Of these 99 were killed during the first postwar governments with Alcide De Gaspari as Prime Minister and Mario Scelba as Minister of the Interior.[6]

However, the compromise of leading Christian Democrats with former Fascist elements is complex and has traditionally been subjected to contrasting interpretations. On Labour Day 1947, for example, the peasants of three villages near Palermo gathered at Portella delle Ginestre to celebrate the notable increase of the People's Bloc in the regional elections, but were met with 15 minutes of sub-machine-gunning. The bandit Salvatore Giuliano reminded in this way the peasants about the true power relations in Sicily regardless of the recent election result.[7] The eventual political hand in the event has never been clear, but there has been much speculation about the terrorist act being sponsored by people from the Christian Democratic ranks and Scelba's ministry. In 1996, new crucial documents were found in a secret deposit on Via Appia. This material indicates that Giuliano had links to clandestine Fascist groups in Italy. Still, the same material also suggests that the terrorist act was probably not planned by Christian Democrats but may well have been directed against them as a warning that they had to outlaw the Communist Party.[8] The fact remains that the Communist Party was expelled from Government on 13 May, when De Gasperi resigned, and remained isolated from government posts for the rest of Cold War, despite being Italy's second largest political party.

In addition, we need only recall the several attempts at a coup d'etat, with links to extreme right-wing political forces, which took place between 1945 and 1989 to understand that democracy was not as well-rooted as one might have hoped for. We need only to ponder on the

---

[5] Paul Ginsborg, *A History of Contemporary History. Society and Politics in Italy 1943-1988*, London: Penguin Books 1990, p. 92.
[6] Nico Perrone, *Il Segno della DC. L'Italia dalla sconfitta al G-7*, Bari: Edizioni Dedalo 2002, p. 5.
[7] Paul Ginsborg, op. cit., pp. 111-112.
[8] Aldo Giannuli, 'Salvatore Giuliano. Un bandito Fascista', *Libertaria*, ottobre/dicembre 2003, pp. 48-58.

1953 election decree, which the opposition named *Legge Truffa* (i.e. the swindle law), comparing it with Mussolini's infamous *Acerbo* law of 1923. We need only to think of the years of extreme left-wing violence and terrorism, which in some cases apparently was countered with terrorism with presumed links to the extreme political right and government circles. In recent years, historians and political scientists on the Left have argued that the execution of the Christian Democratic leader Aldo Moro in 1978, albeit planned and carried out by the Red Brigades, fitted only too well into an overall anti-Communist strategy, known as the "*strategia della tensione*" ('Strategy of Tension'), which aimed to block Aldo Moro's plans for a closer co-operation with the Communists, thus suggesting the existence of some kind of hidden anti-Communist hand in the process. Scholars and intellectuals on the Right have fiercely criticised such interpretations.[9]

If one wishes to understand why Fascism has had some influence in postwar Italy, it is probably not enough to look only at the raison-d'être of the Cold War. Explanations of a mental or psychological character should be taken into consideration as well. The revengeful atmosphere breathed in the last days of April 1945, when people celebrated the fall of the regime and the hanging of the already mutilated bodies of Mussolini, his mistress Claretta Petacci and other exponents of the Social Republic, soon gave way to more complex feelings. Sergio Luzzatto's study of the myths related to the dead body of the *Duce* plausibly argues that the Italians reacted very differently to the execution of the tyrant whom they had once enthusiastically cheered at carefully choreographed public gatherings. In fact, two similar discourses seem to have arisen around the dead corpse of the *Duce*: one laic and pitiful towards the butchers of the past, and another Christian and inclined towards pardoning the dictator and his numerous followers.[10] These circumstances may have favoured the wide acceptance of many

---

[9] See for example Giovanni Pellegrino's Stragi Commission report, cited in Daniele Ganser, *NATO's Secret Armies. Operation Gladio and Terrorism in Western Europe*, London: Frank Cass 2005, pp. 81. See also Giovanni Fasanella, Claudio Sestieri & Giovanni Pellegrini, *Segreto di Stato. La verità da Gladio al caso Moro*, Torino: Einaudi 2000. The various experts who witnessed before the Stragi Commission provided highly contrasting interpretations. Cf. the interrogations of the "Commissione parlamentare d'inchiesta sul terrorismo in Italia e sulle cause della mancata individuazione dei responsabili delle stragi" available on: www.parlamento.it/bicam/terror/home.htm

[10] Cf. Sergio Luzzatto, *Il corpo del duce*, Torino: Einaudi 1998, p. 11.

of the pro-Mussolinian discourses alongside the official anti-Fascist rhetoric.[11]

This brings us to the next question: If what has been briefly stated above can be taken as an indication that Fascism still played some role in Italian society after 1945, then to which extent did it influence intellectual life? And did it have any consequences for the way scholars after 1945 have dealt with Italy's Fascist past and the resistance experience?

During the postwar era, the new political elite and anti-Fascist intellectuals contributed to the creation of a new Italian identity and patriotism. A part of this process was to try to explain to the Italians and to the outside world why it all had gone wrong in the first place. However, in the first postwar analysis of the Fascist regime and its dictator, political battles and personal memoirs largely overshadowed documentary investigation. This was the case even in the fine studies of Gaetano Salvemini, Luigi Salvatorelli, Giovanni Mira and Mario Luciollo.[12] Especially the work of the latter, called *Mussolini e l'Europa* was a truly great book, distinctly anti-Fascist and European in spirit, which still today stands the test of time because of its intellectual honesty. However, the no-doubt most influential Italian scholar of Fascism, Renzo De Felice, clearly dissociated himself from such works. It was actually as a reaction to these works that De Felice undertook the task of writing the first scientific biography of Mussolini. After the Soviet invasion of Hungary in 1956, De Felice had left the Communist Party and began a long journey, not only scientifically (his book on Mussolini would take up the rest of his life until his death in 1996), but also politically.[13]

The fact that De Felice in 1987 made a public appeal for a change of the article of the Italian constitution that prohibits the reconstitution of the Fascist Party *PNF* under any form, contributed to the growing sus-

---

[11] For references, see ibid, pp. 227-228. Another fortunate analysis of the fascist impact in postwar Italy, yet from an entirely different angle, is: Nicola Tranfaglia, *L'Italia repubblicana e l'eredità del fascismo*, Alessandria: Edizioni dell'Orso 2001.

[12] Cf. Mario Luciollo [Mario Donosti], *Mussolini e l'Europa*, Roma/Firenze: Leonardo 1945; Luigi Salvatorelli & Giovanni Mira: *Storia del Fascismo. L'Italia dal 1919 al 1945*, Roma: Novissima 1952. For a positive revaluation of some of these works, see Lucio Ceva, *Guerra Mondiale. Strategie e industria bellica 1939-1945*, Milano: Franco Angeli 2000, pp. 263-284.

[13] The leading Italian scholar of Fascism, Emilio Gentile, has published a minor study of De Felice's academic achievements. Cf. Emilio Gentile, *Renzo De Felice. Lo storico e il personaggio*, Roma-Bari: Laterza, 2003.

picion that his life-long work had not been as impartial as he had always claimed.[14] It rather seemed to have served, his opponents argued, the overriding purpose of legitimising certain political views. However, De Felice maintained until his death that there had been only one guiding principle in his work, namely objectivity based on a sort of *rankian* empiricism (the greatest difference between him and Ranke being that the latter was actually a master of narration and the former a hopeless writer, I might add). In the mid-1990s, De Felice started a debate about whether anti-Fascism could still be seen as the primary key to the understanding of the significance of the Italian Resistance.[15] In his view, anti-Fascism, which was not only the basis of the Italian constitution but had also been the main idea behind many Italian politicians' wish for a still closer European co-operation, was no longer a useful interpretation. De Felice's new challenge to the existing historiography coincided with what has been labelled as the fall of the First Republic, i.e. the disappearance of the Christian Democratic Party, the Communist Party and the Socialist Party, and the rise of the reformed neo-Fascist party, *Alleanza Nazionale*, Silvio Berlusconi's *Forza Italia* and Umberto Bossi's *Lega Nord*. These parties have all expressed themselves negatively about the anti-Fascist experience and often promoted anti-European views, which are in direct conflict with the ideas of the founding fathers of the Italian Republic.

It was also in this period following the fall of the Berlin Wall that precious but hitherto hermetically closed archives across the world were suddenly opened to the public. All this new material led to a much-needed historical debate about Italian identity and its close relation with the resistance movement, traditionally presented as a 'second *Risorgimento*'. The polemics were mainly centred on the last two years of the Second World War and on the important political events of the immediate postwar era. Due to the thorough historical research of the 1990s, in particular Lutz Klinkhammer's path-breaking study of the Republic of Salò, there is now a growing consensus among historians that Mussolini's social republic in North Italy was much more than a Fascist satellite blindly obeying the *Reich*.[16] Thanks to the sharp analysis of Claudio Pavone from 1992, we all now speak of the last two

---

[14] Carl Levy, 'Historians and the First Republic', in Stefan Berger, Mark Donovan & Kevin Passmore (eds.), *Writing National Histories. Western Europe since 1800*, London: Routledge 1999, pp.265-269.

[15] Renzo De Felice, *Rosso e nero*, Milano: Baldini & Castoldi 1995, pp. 17, 24-25.

[16] Lutz Klinkhammer, *L'occupazione tedesca in Italia 1943-1945*, Torino: Bollati Boringhieri 1993. See also Levy, op. cit.

years of the war in Italy as the Italian Civil War, as a class-war and as a patriotic war, in which the myth of violence was not an exclusivity of the Republic of Salò, but rather a general phenomenon of the whole war.[17]

More important, in the 1990s historians inside and outside the Defelician paradigm began to question the sincerity of the democratic and responsible policy line undertaken by the Italian Communist Party during the Civil War. De Felice, Rusconi, Colletti, Sechi, Aga Rossi and others have questioned the sincerity of the so-called 'svolta di Salerno' of 1944, when Communist leader Palmiro Togliatti upon his return from Moscow declared that he was willing to respect the rules of democracy. Numerous studies have argued that the patriotic and independent line followed by Togliatti was instrumental, if not directly dictated by Stalin. As an unavoidable consequence of the post-1989 breakdown of the Italian Communist Party, which had played a crucial role in the Italian resistance, a new historiographical trend emerged. The professed purpose of this new school was to deconstruct the "myths" of anti-Fascism and Communism. The question of the 1990s, as recalled by Carl Levy, were hence: if all democrats by definition are anti-Fascists, would it then be fair to conclude that all anti-Fascists by definition were democrats?[18] By posing this question, several historians and opinion makers were hinting at the fact that the democratic credentials of the Communist Party, the dominant force within the anti-Fascist resistance, had only been instrumental. Others pointed out that the commitment of the Communist Party to fight nazism/Fascism had been impeccable, albeit some elements of the party probably saw the resistance as a real opportunity to settle the accounts with the dominating Italian classes. Despite the duplicity, which can certainly be registered in some of Togliatti's statements, the Italian anti-Fascist experience of the Civil War probably strengthened the democratic profile and independent line of the party in the decades to come. After Khruschev's revelations of the Stalinist purges in 1956, Togliatti took the chance of denouncing Stalin and demanding freedom of action for individual European Communist parties, a so-called polycentric partysystem. On the other hand, this proposal also shows the strategic abilities and highly developed instinct of survival that Togliatti possessed. As Vice-Secretary of the Comintern in the 1930s, he must have been,

---

[17] Claudio Pavone, *Una guerra civile. Saggio storico sulla moralità nella Resistenza* I-II, Turin: Bollato Boringhieri, 1994.
[18] See Levy, op. cit., pp. 265-269.

at the very least, acquainted with Stalin's dictatorial practices.[19] Hence, one might certainly say that his denouncement of the Stalinist crimes came rather late, and during the Hungarian Revolution, the PCI leaders supported the Soviet invasion. The Christian Democratic leader Aldo Moro has stressed that regardless of these duplicities, one should never forget that the Communist Party was an important part of the ideals and the political and cultural choices of the Italian people.[20] Culturally, one might add, the greatest mistake of the PCI in the postwar era was probably its tendency to monopolise the anti-Fascist experience of the Second World War, with the inevitable consequence that people who did not share the Communist interpretation, had great difficulties identifying with anti-Fascism as a universal and important pillar of the new-born democracy.

The devaluation of the resistance movement is particular manifest in the works of Renzo De Felice, who saw the arrest of Mussolini in 1943 and the following armistice as a truly tragic event for the country. He considered the division of Italy into two blocs, the Republic of Salò obeying the *Reich*, and a southern reign fighting together with the allies, as the nadir of National history, because it meant the end of the House of Savoy, the dissolution of the Armed forces and the end of Italian autonomy. So, what according to traditional historiography was a war of liberation, a second *risorgimento* aiming to throw out the German occupying forces, was for De Felice a civil war of Italians loyal to the regime in the south and Italians loyal to the regime in the north. Where, according to the anti-Fascist interpretation, it was necessary to "demonize" the Republic of Salò in order to promote anti-Fascism, democratic values and international co-operation in the new Republic, De Felice sustained that the fierce criticism served another purpose, namely that of hiding the existence of a wide-spread sense of patriotism in the north.[21] Even though one may certainly accept a part of the Defelician thesis, it becomes increasingly difficult to understand his subsequent arguments. In fact, it seems that in the process of deconstructing the myth of the Left, he has contributed to the creation of what I would define as a counter-mythology of the right.[22]

---

[19] Ginsborg, op. cit, p. 205.
[20] Gert Sørensen, 'Il caso Moro e il potere sovrano', *Studi Storici*. no. 4, ottobre-dicembre 2002, anno 43, p. 1077.
[21] De Felice op. cit., pp. 11-12 and note 2.
[22] For a critical view of De Felice "anti-antiFascism" see MacGregor Knox, 'The Fascist Regime, its Foreign Policy and its Wars: an 'Anti-antiFascist' Orthodoxy?', *Contemporary European History*, 4:3, 1995. See also Morten Heiberg, *Emperado-*

According to De Felice, Mussolini had only the most humble and noble motives for accepting the leadership of the Republic of Salò: "Mussolini, whether you like it or not, accepted Hitler's proposal encouraged by a patriotic motivation: a true and real 'sacrifice' on the Altar of the Defence of Italy".[23] We may certainly add that this conclusion cannot find any support in the available evidence.[24] This is after all remarkable for a historian, who rated empiricism above all other scientific principles. Rather the idea owes to a book published in 1947 by Quinto Navarra, who was allegedly Mussolini's butler. The real authorship of this peculiar book has been attributed to two Italian intellectuals, who at first had backed the Fascist regime, but later crossed over to the anti-Fascist side.[25] The two presumed authors, Montanelli and Longanesi, tried to present Mussolini as a humble patriot serving only the best interest of the *Patria*. This myth, created by one of the most unreliable books to be published in the aftermath of the Second World War, played a major role in the rehabilitation of Fascism in Italy. Regardless of who actually produced the memories of butler Navarra, few books have been as influential as this one. Almost all of those who write about Mussolini afterwards use it, albeit they do not quote it directly.[26]

Klinkhammer's study has demonstrated that there was not much heroism in Mussolini's choice to accept Hitler's proposal. It is beyond doubt that Mussolini's room for action was simply an unexpected by-product of the eternal hatred and clashes between the different German commanders in North Italy.[27] Also problematic was De Felice's appraisal of Commander Junio Valerio Borghese, one of the foremost exponents of the Salò-Republic, but according to De Felice "difficult to consider a Fascist. The reason that brought him to [North Italy] on the side of Mussolini, and not to Pescara, on the side of the King, was the defence of the intangibility of the territory and above all the idea of restoring Italy to its national honour lost by the 'treachery of 8 September' 1943".[28] According to this line of interpretation, Borghese had

---

res del Mediterráneo. Mussolini, Franco y la guerra civil española, Barcelona: Crítica 2003, chapter 2.
[23] De Felice, op. cit., p. 114.
[24] See also Aurelio Lepre, *Mussolini*, Bari: Laterza 1998, pp. 118-119.
[25] According to Luzzatto the authors were Indro Montanelli and Longanesi (1947).
[26] Ceva, op. cit., p. 265.
[27] Klinkhammer, op. cit., p. 420.
[28] De Felice, op.cit., p. 128. For an analysis of the international aspects of the armistice, see Elena Aga Rossi, *Una nazione allo sbando. L'armistizio italiano del settembre 1943*, Bologna: Il Mulino: 1993 (revised edition 1998).

been a true patriot, because he fought a fierce battle to reduce Tito's influence in the region of Venezia-Giulia. The fact that Borghese in the postwar period was aligned with the extreme political right and even conducted a failed military coup in 1970 is ignored in De Felice's evaluation of the man's integrity and benign intentions.

In sum, in the 1990s, a new literature was born in Italy, which openly defined itself as revisionist and which tended to put everything into discussion which had been achieved in the name of anti-Fascism, from the resistance to the constitution of a democratic republic to the joining of the European Union. Revisionism becomes *salonfähig* not only among professional historians, but also in the newspapers which see a unique chance to trigger political discussions over past historical experiences. This revisionism is probably part of a much wider European historiographical-philosophical current, represented in Germany by Ernst Nolte and in France by Francois Furet. The common denominator of this European revisionism is that it sees the European Jacobin culture, the so-called 'immortal principles of 1789', as the main responsible of the infernal violence of the 20th century.[29] As an example of this line of interpretation, we may mention the 1998 polemics provoked by the former Italian Ambassador to the Soviet Union Sergio Romano, who sustained that those Italians who in 1938 went to Spain to help the Spanish dictator Franco defeat the Republic did well, because the opponent regime was turning into a Soviet satellite.[30] In the following weeks, the debate spread to half a dozen other European countries, despite the fact that Romano's thesis was based on a completely erroneous analysis of Soviet power in Spain.[31]

It was also in the 1990s that the discussions about the role of the *Patria* reached a new peak. Italian historian Ernesto Galli della Loggia sustained in a highly controversial book that the 45 days from Mussolini's arrest in July 1943 to 8 September, the day of the Italian Armistice, led to nothing less than the death of the *Patria*. In his view, anti-Fascist historians have ignored the fact that initially Italy was amputated geographically by its allies and the Peace Treaty of 1947, which conceded land to France, Yugoslavia and Greece. Accordingly, the anti-Fascist resistance led to the creation of an 'Anti-national Partitoc-

---

[29] Cf. Domenico Losurdo, *Il revisionismo storico. Problemi e miti*, Roma/Bari: Laterza 1998, pp. 3-7.
[30] The second edition of the book by Nino Isaio et al. has gathered all the main interventions during the Italian 'Historikerstreit'. Nino Isaia & Edgardo Sogno (eds.), *Due fronti. La grande polemica sulla guerra di Spagna*, Firenze: libri liberal 1998.
[31] Heiberg, op. cit., p. x, 70-72.

racy', in which the Christian Democrats allowed the nation-state to erode by giving preference to Catholic internationalism and to the integration of Italy into NATO and the European Community: "The Republic has never been able to become *Patria*, and Democracy has never been able to meet with the Nation."[32] Galli Della Loggia and fellow historians Giovanni Sabbatucci, Giovanni Belardelli and Luciano Cafagna further lament that the Italians have been morally deprived of their capital Rome, which now only exists as a negative phenomenon in the minds of the Italians. The ghost of Rome, Belardelli writes, "has continued until this day to dominate the public discourse of the Italians, but now only with a negative accent".[33] Bearing Mussolini's 1932-speech in mind, one certainly feels entitled to ask the following question: how would it have been possible for the Italian leaders in the aftermath of the Second World War to celebrate the national or patriotic value of Rome, symbol if not the incarnation of the aggressive nationalism of the irresponsible Duce, who in the name of the eternal city had fought no less than five wars in twenty years? The idea of the Christian Democrats to deliberately associate Rome with peace and international co-operation seems to me to have been an intelligent and well-pondered choice.

The criticism against the parties of the First Republic also fails to understand the continuity between the clientelistic practices of the Fascist regime and the way of doing in the *partitocrazia* of the postwar period. Surprisingly, the DC policies of justice, family and work present considerable elements of continuity. State intervention in industry was one of the most important bases for the consolidation of the *partitocrazia*, yet it was not invented by the Christian Democrats. It was created by Mussolini, who in this way managed to create consensus among the crisis-ridden industrialists for his own regime. The main difference between the Fascist era and the 1950s was that the IRI and other public holding companies created during Fascism became efficient instruments for the modernization of the Italian industry and for the reintegration of Italy into the international economy, something which led to a considerable, if not miraculous increase in the living standards in Italy.[34]

---

[32] Ernesto Galli della Loggia, *La morte della Patria: la crisi dell'idea di nazione tra Resistenza, antiFascismo e Repubblica*, Roma/Bari: Laterza 1996, p. 137

[33] Giovanni Belardelli, Ernesto Galli della Loggia, Giovanni Sabbatucci &Luciano Cafagna, *Miti e storia dell'Italia unita*, Bologna: Il Mulino 1999, p. 19.

[34] See Levy, op. cit.

When interrogated by the *Stragi* Commission in 1997, Giulio Andreotti could rightfully state that despite all the set-backs and the bloodshed Italy had experienced since 1945, which in part was due to the country's Fascist legacy, democracy had after all prevailed: "La democrazia in questo paese ha tenuto".[35] The Christian Democrats had together with their minor political allies rebuilt Italy from the ground and created one of the largest economies in the world. However, the methods employed to achieve this goal had in part been corruption, clientelism and use of state funds, banks and welfare state measures to maintain the electorate and hegemonic status of the Christian Democratic Party complete.[36] During the 1992 corruption scandal called 'Mani Pulite' all this came to a sudden end, and the old parties disappeared. Accordingly, the *Lega Nord*, and to some extent also *Forza Italia* built their popularity on a proclaimed 'rottura' or 'break' with the traditional and corrupt politics of Rome. However, this did not prevent these two new parties from collaborating with the reformed neo-Fascist party, *Alleanza Nazionale*, which, in line with Mussolini's *PNF*, had a much more positive view of the myth of Rome. And, like their predecessors of the First Republic and of the Fascist era, Silvio Berlusconi and other exponents of the new political elite of North Italy soon learned, despite declarations of the opposite, to appreciate Rome as a centre of power, and legislation *ad personam*.

---

[35] Interrogation of Giulio Andreotti by the 'Commissione parlamentare d'inchiesta sul terrorismo in Italia e sulle cause della mancata individuazione dei responsabili delle stragi', Friday 11 april 1997. Cf.
http://www.senato.it/parlam/bicam/terror/stenografici/steno13.htm
[36] Perrone, op. cit., p. 6.

CHAPTER 6

FRANCE'S ROLE IN THE WORLD IN 1945

Back to the Future?

Bent Boel

How did the French decision-makers envision their country's role in the world in 1945? Were they fixated on a glorious past, hoping out of nostalgia to re-establish their country's *grandeur* and stubbornly following a counterproductive – anti-German and Soviet-friendly - policy doomed to failure? Or were they already peering into the future, clear-headedly assessing the new geopolitical situation created by the war, devising an appropriate strategy which would be vindicated a few years later? For many years, most accounts of French foreign policy during the immediate post-war period leaned towards the first thesis. More recently, an alternative narrative has gained ground. French decision-makers appeared tough on Germany mainly for domestic political reasons. Early on they realized that the Soviet threat was bigger than the German one. They were keenly aware of the fact that Germany could not be kept down by coercion. A more constructive solution would have to be found, and Germany would have to be integrated into a Western framework, bolstering the West in its confrontation with the Soviet bloc. Domestic political concerns, however, induced them to follow a double-faced policy: the official anti-German one was obfuscating the real one, which was preparing for the inevitable future compromises. While there is much to be said in favor of the latter thesis, at least as a sound corrective to the somewhat simplistic picturing of a purely obstructionist and anti-German policy supposedly followed at least until 1947/48, it remains difficult to date precisely the French change of heart. To what extent may it be said to have taken place as early as 1945? This article will examine the French policy in four interrelated areas – France's relationship with Germany, the Soviet Union, the United States as well as its plans for European cooperation – and investigate whether the French policy in 1945 was pre-figuring policies later to be followed or was stuck in a futile rearguard battle.[1]

The Situation in 1945: A Weaker France

On the eve of the Second World War, France, while having lost much of its former luster, remained a major world power in charge of an immense colonial empire. Six years later, the colonies were not yet gone, but the situation had been dramatically altered. The two dominating powers not only in the world but also on the European continent were (totally or largely) non-European ones, namely the United States and the Soviet Union. Though the weakening of France's international standing obviously long predated the Second World War, the sudden, crushing and humiliating defeat of 1940 did much to accelerate it. The country remained occupied for four years, the first two partially, the last two in its entirety, and republican institutions were replaced by Marshal Pétain's Vichy regime, which instigated a policy of active collaboration with Nazi Germany while pursuing a reactionary 'national revolution' on the home front. When France was liberated in 1944 the leader of the Free French, General Charles de Gaulle, took over – backed by all the forces which had opposed Vichy. This included the resistance active in France, i.e., a large array of movements, among which the Communist Party (PCF) from 1941 onwards played a major role. In addition, it comprised the Free French, based first in London and later in Algiers, led by de Gaulle who had established himself as a vocal spokesman of French resistance as early as June 1940 and as its unrivalled leader from November 1943. At the Liberation in 1944, however, a number of dangers seemed to lurk. There was much apprehension among some French about their country being put under allied military administration, the so-called AMGOT (Allied Military Government of Occupied Territory) regime. Though the Americans in fact had not made such plans, they deliberately kept the French in the dark

---

[1] Dietmar Hüser, 'Charles de Gaulle, Georges Bidault, Robert Schuman et l'Allemagne 1944-1950. Conceptions, actions, perceptions', *Francia*, Vol. 23, No. 3, 1996, pp. 49-73; Michael Creswell and Marc Trachtenberg, 'France and the German Question, 1945-1955', *Journal of Cold War Studies*, Vol. 5, No. 3, Summer 2003, pp. 5-28.

about their future status.² De Gaulle played a key role in establishing an independent French authority in liberated France, gathering support from all resistance movements and convincing the Western Allies that he was their best hope of keeping the French communists under control. Moreover, de Gaulle managed to unite the French, not only by gaining support from the PCF and other parties but also much more broadly by convincing the French that, save a few traitors, they had all been on the same side, resisting the Germans – if not in acts then at least in their minds. Fears of civil war and of a communist takeover thus rapidly subsided.³

In May 1944, de Gaulle had established a provisional government in which all major political forces participated, including representatives from the three biggest parties: the PCF, the socialists (SFIO) and the newly created Christian Democratic party (MRP). Though this was a national consensus government, de Gaulle's powerful position and immense prestige made him the pivotal decision-maker as far as French foreign policy was concerned. However, he had to maneuver in a transitional and unstable context, with increasing tensions between himself and the parties on the Left, and he had to reckon with the strong communist influence as well as fierce anti-German feelings in the population.⁴ De Gaulle's strength was thus built on a politically fragile foundation.

France was economically and financially weakened. Means of transportation, ports, houses and factories had been destroyed during the war, assets had been removed by the Germans and malnutrition was said to be widespread. In 1945 French GDP was about half of what it had been just before the war. There was a need for reconstruction, both for socio-economic reasons and as a pre-condition for France regaining an international role worthy of its ambitions. French decision-makers identified the steel industry as the key sector for economic modernization. Since rebuilding the steel industry required large quantities of coal, the need for secure and regular coal supplies became a French obsession in these years. Moreover, in 1945 the balance of trade had a deficit of 860 million dollars, and the situation was worsening. France

---

² Régine Torrent, *La France américaine. Controverses de la Libération*, Paris 2004, p. 221; André Kaspi, *La liberation de la France, juin 1944 – janvier 1946*, Paris 2004, pp. 52-53.
³ Philippe Buton, *La Joie douloureuse. La libération de la France*, Bruxelles 2004, pp. 134, 154.
⁴ Pierre Gerbet, *Le relèvement 1944-1949*, Paris 1991, p. 14; Hüser, *Charles de Gaulle*, pp. 55-56.

badly needed dollars to finance its imports, for which reason it hoped for American aid. Though it did receive assistance (until August 1945 under the Lend-Lease program, then as loans), it was far from enough.[5]

Finally, France's international status had been severely damaged by the war, politically, morally and militarily. It was only in October 1944 that the US finally decided to recognize the French provisional government, a gesture on which de Gaulle dismissively commented that the French government appreciated being called by its proper name. Washington, however, remained wary of de Gaulle and of a government in which the communists were represented. France's lack of military clout also limited its international influence. The forces at the disposal of the Free French had been very modest. After the Liberation, France's army expanded rapidly and by May 1945 it numbered 1.3 million people. While this may sound impressive, it was small compared to what the Soviet Union, the US and the UK could muster. During meetings between the three big powers, Soviet, American and British leaders would refer to the modest French contribution to the defeat of the Axis Powers. Stalin was particularly contemptuous of the French performance during the war. Throughout 1945 they held several summit meetings – at Yalta in February, at Potsdam in July-August – without inviting the French and despite the fact that they discussed questions, in particular relating to Germany, in which the French had a major interest. In many ways, France in 1945 depended on support from allies which were reluctant to accept it as an equal partner. This situation created frustration and bitterness in Paris.[6]

Betting on the Future: A Greater France?

At first sight, and certainly seen from the perspective of the world's two major powers, France in 1945 had much to be modest about and could have been expected to show some restraint in its international behavior. French decision-makers – and in particular General de Gaulle – saw things quite differently. Despite the seeming weakness of their country, they had ambitious foreign policy goals. They believed

---

[5] René Girault, 'La France est-elle une grande puissance en 1945?', Maurice Vaisse (ed.), *8 mai 1945. La victoire en Europe*, Paris 2005, p. 98; Gérard Bossuat, *La France, l'aide américaine et la construction européenne 1944-1954*, vol. 1, Paris 1997, pp. 40-41. Research presented by Professor Hein Klemann at the conference "1945 – Back to Normal or New Beginning?" (Copenhagen Business School, 29-30 September 2005) demonstrates that commonly accepted figures about the destructions caused by the Second World War should not necessarily be trusted.

[6] Girault, 'La France est-elle une grande puissance en 1945?', p. 94; André Kaspi, *La libération de la France, juin 1944 – janvier 1946*, Paris 2004, pp. 255-56.

makers. Admittedly, some feared that an overly anti-German policy might prove counterproductive and therefore favored a more cooperative approach. Some even insisted on the need for a European framework within which to solve the German problem. However, in 1945 the coercive approach dominated.[12] There is some – ambiguous – evidence suggesting that Georges Bidault, foreign minister during de Gaulle's premiership as well as afterwards, may not really have believed in his own anti-German rhetoric or in the realism of France's demands in relationship to Germany. Rather he clung to these positions mainly for domestic political reasons. However that may be, that same evidence also confirms the depth of de Gaulle's feelings about Germany. In August 1946, Bidault distanced himself from France's German policy but blamed it on de Gaulle from whom he had inherited it and whose ideas remained popular among French voters.[13] Furthermore, French insistence in 1945 on excluding Germany from a European customs union was not caused by domestic political concerns but by the genuine French aspiration to take over Germany's leading economic role on the European continent, an ambition which presupposed that Germany to some degree could be kept "down". As late as 1948, France's German policy, regardless of the misgivings which decision-makers like Bidault may have had, was still viewed by the US as being "outmoded and unrealistic".[14]

The Russian Card

The Soviet Union presented France both with an opportunity and with a challenge. For historians, an important issue has been to determine at what stage French decision-makers began identifying the Russian threat as a major problem which ought to be taken even more seriously than the German one. In 1945, the Soviet menace appeared far from salient to everybody. The prevailing mood in France was friendly to the Soviet Union due to its immense contribution to the defeat of Nazi Germany, and it took several years before these sentiments evaporated. The 'revisionist' approach has argued that French decision-makers ear-

---

[12] Georges-Henri Soutou, 'Le deuil de la puissance (1914-1958)', Jean-Claude Allain et al., *Histoire de la diplomatie française*, Paris 2005, p. 808.
[13] Michael Creswell and Marc Trachtenberg, 'France and the German Question, 1945-1955', *Journal of Cold War Studies*, Vol. 5, No. 3, Summer 2003, p. 11. See also: Michael Creswell and Marc Trachtenberg, 'New Light on an Old Issue?', *Journal of Cold War Studies*, Vol. 5, No. 3, Summer 2003, p. 51.
[14] Creswell and Trachtenberg, 'France and the German Question', p. 15; Gérard Bossuat, *L'Europe des Français 1943-1959*, Paris 1996, pp. 41-43.

lier than usually accepted (i.e., in 1945 rather than in 1947/48) did perceive the Soviet Union as a major (or even the main) threat. Initially, however, they – and de Gaulle in particular – certainly saw the Soviet Union as a card which could be used to improve France's international position. De Gaulle's motivations were mainly geopolitical. He was a realist and he believed that what mattered in international politics were states rather than ideologies. To de Gaulle, the Soviet Union was just a cover for eternal Russia.[15] Close relations with the Soviet Union in his view served a triple purpose, two of which related to foreign policy, the last one reflecting domestic political concerns. First, the good old "alliance de revers" which would face Germany with the threat of war on two fronts, in the west with France, in the east with the Soviet Union. Another purpose was to strengthen French hands vis-à-vis the 'Anglo-Saxons', primarily the Americans. De Gaulle wanted to use his relations with the Russians to compensate for his heavy reliance on the British and the Americans. Finally, the domestic political purpose was to help keep the PCF in line.[16]

The importance which de Gaulle attached to the Russian alliance was attested by the long and strenuous trip he embarked upon in December 1944 when he went to Moscow to negotiate with Stalin. His efforts seemed crowned with success when the two leaders signed a 20-year alliance directed against any potential German threat. However, there was a catch with this treaty. The French were much more eager to sign it than the Russians were. Moscow had originally envisioned something looser; it was the French who had insisted on a stronger commitment. This enabled the Russians to make the French pay a heavy price, namely what amounted to a de facto recognition of the communist Lublin government in Poland at a time when other Western countries still insisted that the exiled Polish government in London was the sole legitimate one. Given France's traditional close ties with Poland, this concession was an important one. Stalin on his part made no serious overtures to the French. That de Gaulle had good reasons to be disappointed was confirmed in the following months, as evidence accumulated indicating that Stalin did not care much about French interests. Rather, he actively undermined them, refusing to back French claims in Germany and opposing to award France a zone of occupation. Partly in reaction to the failure of his Russian policy and prompted by a growing fear of the perceived Soviet threat, de Gaulle

---

[15] Creswell and Trachtenberg, 'New Light on an Old Issue?', p. 47; Buton, *La joie douloureuse,* pp. 160-61.
[16] Young, 'France's European Policy', p. 441.

initiated by mid-1945 a *rapprochement* with Washington, and in September 1945 he reiterated his 1944 proposal for a Western European Bloc. He also made it clear that France did not want the Soviet Union to gain any significant presence in the Western occupied zones of Germany. At this stage French hopes that the Soviet Union would be a help in matters relating to the German problem had been laid to rest.[17] However, the French still hoped to avoid a confrontation between East and West, to some degree even to play a role as bridge-builder, and this policy cannot be satisfactorily explained by purely domestic concerns. It was a genuine French goal in these years to avoid an escalation in the Cold War which could have dangerous consequences on the European continent.[18]

The American Challenge

It would take more than twenty years before the expression "the American challenge" became popular in France and elsewhere, through the publication of Jean-Jacques Servan-Schreiber's book carrying that same title. However, the French did feel challenged by the Americans in 1945. At the end of the war America was the great European power, supplanting among others France, and it represented a successful economic model at a time when French decision-makers felt that their own social and economic system was seriously deficient. They knew that they needed American economic assistance. But they wanted to remain sovereign – and even more: they wanted to regain their international position. Their self-assigned task was thus to benefit from American aid without losing their independence.[19]

The Franco-American relationship was thus ambivalent. On the one hand, the American role in liberating France had created a link of gratitude and even admiration. In addition, for both political and economic reasons French decision-makers wished to see the United States remain involved in European matters. But other more mixed feelings played a role as well. During the war de Gaulle's relationship with the Americans, and in particular with President Franklin Roosevelt, had

---

[17] Georges-Henri Soutou, 'General de Gaulle and the Soviet Union, 1943-5: Ideology or European Equilibrium', Francesca Gori and Silvio Pons (eds.), *The Soviet Union and Europe in the Cold War*, London 1996, pp. 310-333.

[18] Bent Boel, 'La France, les Etats-Unis et la politique occidentale d'embargo, 1948-1954', *Revue d'histoire diplomatique*, No. 1, 2001, p. 37.

[19] Robert Frank, 'Le dilemme français: La modernisation sous influence ou l'indépendance dans la decadence', René Girault and Robert Frank (eds.), *La puissance française en question, 1945-1949*, Paris 1988, pp. 146-47.

been tense. Roosevelt mistrusted de Gaulle's democratic credentials and for a brief period in 1943 backed his rival in Algiers, General Henri Giraud. Though the latter was soon completely marginalized, de Gaulle remained keenly aware of his own vulnerability, and for that very reason he would often take an uncompromising stand in his dealings with the Americans. He felt that any concession might be interpreted as a sign of weakness that he could not afford. The fact that Roosevelt died in April 1945 and was replaced by Truman may have helped improve relations. In any case, soon afterwards the US State Department favored giving up Roosevelt's contemptuous treatment of de Gaulle because it recognized that France was vital for US policy in Europe and that de Gaulle represented the best safeguard against the French communists.[20]

Other problems remained though. The Americans were initially greeted as liberators, but in many cases relations between American troops and the local French population grew sour.[21] More fundamental was the dependency created by the inequality between the two countries. As the French financial situation worsened, it became ever clearer that in the short and medium term France was bound to be heavily reliant on Washington for economic assistance. France did receive some help in 1945, but far from enough to solve its problems. Moreover, as early as 1945 some decision-makers realized that if France was to modernize, then it would have to learn from the US and at least to some extent try to emulate American ways of doing things. This would later lead to the so-called productivity drive with the French and other Western Europeans trying to uncover the secrets behind the US success.[22]

In August 1945, de Gaulle went to the US, in an attempt to improve Franco-American relations. Several considerations may explain this move. Threat perceptions – i.e., persistent preoccupation with the German problem as well as a growing concern about Soviet behavior – played their part. But economic motivations were central. The French hoped to secure financial loans as well as coal supplies from the

---

[20] Robert Dallek, 'Roosevelt and De Gaulle', Robert Paxton and Nicholas Wahl, *De Gaulle and the United States. A Centennial Reappraisal*, Oxford 1994, pp. 49-52; Young, 'France's European Policy', p. 442.

[21] Thierry de Montbrial, 'Franco-American Relations: A Historical-Structural Analysis,' *Cambridge Review of International Affairs*, Vol. 17, No. 3, October 2004, p. 460.

[22] Bent Boel, *The European Productivity Agency and Transatlantic Relations, 1953-1961*, Copenhagen 2003, pp. 21-59.

Americans. During the discussions geopolitical and economic factors got mixed up. While French views on the Soviet threat had evolved, the French also realized that the best way to impress the Americans favorably was to present France as a barrier to communism.[23]

A European Solution?

Finally, two European options were contemplated by the French decision-makers: a British alliance and Western European cooperation. During the exile years the Free French expected that France and Great Britain would move towards a close alliance. At the end of the war, however, a number of problems stood in the way for such a development. Conflicts about the German policy played a central role – thus confirming the importance which the French attached to that issue – but other issues also troubled the relationship, in particular in the Middle East. For that reason, it was not before 1947 that the French and the British were able to sign the Dunkirk Treaty.[24]

While in Algiers, 1943-44, the Free French discussed a number of options involving the creation of a Western European community, the membership and nature of which varied from one draft to another. The most daring of these plans was Jean Monnet's idea to create a European entity uniting the big steelproducing regions in the center of Europe (including both German and French regions). De Gaulle did not accept Monnet's proposal but in March 1944 he aired the idea of some sort of European co-operation. The overall goal was to create a framework allowing France to play a leading role in Western Europe (thus helping to ensure a multilateral control of Germany) while prompting the modernization of French industry. The plan failed for a number of reasons, major ones being Belgian and especially Dutch reluctance to enter into a customs union with France which excluded the British and the Germans. Moreover, the Soviets saw the scheme as one directed against them and protested vehemently each time de Gaulle mentioned the Western bloc idea. The Americans at this stage disapproved of the idea of creating a regional economic bloc. So, at least initially, nothing came of the French plans aimed a creating a Western bloc or a customs union.[25]

---

[23] Young, 'France's European Policy', pp. 445-446.
[24] Soutou, 'De Gaulle's Plans for Postwar Europe', pp. 52-53.
[25] Bossuat, *L'Europe des Français*, pp. 23-51; Young, 'France's European Policy', pp. 440-41.

Achievements

What did the foreign policy adopted by France at the end of the Second World War achieve? At first sight, not much. As far as the number one problem, Germany, was concerned, the French had difficulties making themselves heard at all. They were excluded from the crucial meetings at Yalta and Potsdam. At Potsdam, the Big Three had adopted a position quite opposite the French one, stating that Germany should remain united and more particularly opposing any detachment of the Ruhr and the Rhineland. At the Council of Foreign Ministers meeting following Potsdam, they refused to listen to French complaints. Instead, France was invited to contact the Big Three on a bilateral basis. The French obliged, visiting in turn London (in October), Washington (in November) and Moscow (in December). These talks only served to highlight the other problem which the French were facing, namely that none of the other occupying powers were ready to support their claims towards Germany. The Americans felt that after its crushing defeat Germany no longer constituted a threat. On the contrary, they were concerned about its economic viability and political stability. Moreover, they opposed letting the Soviets into the Ruhr through the establishment of an international authority such as the one advocated by the French. The British had similar concerns. The Soviets favored establishing an international control over the Ruhr since this solution would provide them with a say in matters concerning a key German region, something which the Americans and British were determined to prevent, and which the French themselves were getting wary of. In German matters the French were isolated and seemed to be getting nowhere.[26]

Moreover, the cards which the French thought they had at their disposal to advance their interests had not served them well. Most blatantly, the Russian strategy failed because Moscow proved unwilling to play its part in the game proposed by de Gaulle. Stalin did nothing to help the French or to give any substance to the Franco-Soviet treaty. Perhaps because, as an American diplomat pointed out, he had no wish to help establish another major power on the European continent.[27] As far as the US was concerned, the French hoped for assistance while insisting on protecting their own sovereignty. Some American help was forthcoming, but not nearly as much as the French were hoping for. At

---

[26] Young, 'France's European Policy', pp. 443, 448.
[27] Georges-Henri Soutou, 'De Gaulle's Plans for Postwar Europe', Antonio Varsori and Elena Calandri (eds.), *The Failure of Peace in Europe*, 1943-1948, New York, 2002, p. 57.

the same time, the French and the Americans had a number of conflicts. For instance, in May-June 1945 France's occupation of the Italian region Val d'Aosta almost led the US to end all military supplies to France. And throughout this period the Americans were a major obstacle to achieving French goals in Germany. The demonstratively independent policy followed by de Gaulle isolated France vis-à-vis its Western allies and the increasing East-West tensions were narrowing the French room for maneuver. Finally, the European option did not appear very promising either. None of the French plans for Western Europe were implemented in 1945 and endeavors to establish a Franco-British alliance failed because of the low priority given to that option by the French and because of numerous disagreements between the two countries. To all these shortcomings one could add the ominous policy aiming at re-establishing the French empire which in the following years would prove extremely costly, both politically, economically, and in terms of human life.[28]

One may argue that the French policy was doomed to failure from the outset. There was a huge discrepancy between the ambitious goals formulated by de Gaulle and France's diplomatic, political, military and economic resources. In addition, de Gaulle even had difficulties on the domestic front, since the priority he gave to his foreign policy goals was not wholeheartedly backed by all the big political parties. In some respects, then, the policy followed in 1945 was revealing itself to be a dead-end.[29]

However, this is not the whole story. On the domestic front the political and technocratic elites taking over at the Liberation had laid the first foundations for the subsequent decades' impressive economic growth and modernization allowing General de Gaulle to give some substance to a very active and outspoken foreign policy in the 1960es. For instance, it was in December 1945 that de Gaulle, prompted by Jean Monnet, decided to create the General Planning Commission. Moreover, against many odds, France had managed to preserve some degree of international status, both symbolically and formally. In particular, it had gained a permanent seat in the United Nations Security Council, an occupation zone in Germany and a seat in the Allied Control Council established to oversee the four occupation zones in Germany. After Potsdam the French were represented on the Council of Foreign Ministers, the body established to agree on the future peace

---

[28] Jacques Marseille, *Empire colonial et capitalisme français*, Paris 1984, p. 367.
[29] Kaspi, *La liberation de la France,* p. 421.

treaties. In other words, France had managed to become the fourth member of the Big Three. These positive results may sometimes have owed less to French policies than to its Western allies' – and in particular the UK's – interest in boosting France's position in relationship to both Germany and the Soviet Union.[30] However, one may argue that France's vehement insistence on respect for its rights and status played a role as well. And the blackmail of the weak, which French decision-makers started using already in 1945, would subsequently prove quite successful, when they would often bemoan the vulnerability of the Fourth Republic's governments, and in particular highlight the communist threat, in order to strengthen their bargaining position with the Americans. While it took some time for France to get the assistance it asked for, it wounded up ranking number two among the European recipients of Marshall Aid, and French planners proved quite adept at putting the American assistance to uses defined by themselves.

In several ways, French decision-makers in 1945 anticipated policies which would later be developed more fully. This applies to the more forward-looking aspects of French post-war policy. Indeed, the many diverse plans about European co-operation together with the early understanding of a need to give the Germans hope would later come to fruition in the Schuman Plan and the ensuing process of European integration. By clinging to that idea, France would eventually find a constructive solution to the German problem, a framework for her own economic growth and modernization as well as a way to play a leading role on the European continent during the Cold War. However, it also applies to those aspects of the French policy which have subsequently been derided as out of tune with the changed international situation at the end of the Second World War but which to some degree reflected more permanent French foreign policy preoccupations. The French insistence on *grandeur* and independence was not just backward-looking nostalgia. It reflected aspirations which would inspire French post-war foreign policy, particularly during de Gaulle's presidency in the 1960s, but also afterwards. French fears of Germany and the related temptation to play the Russian card to counterbalance such a potential threat have continued to play a role in French post-war policy as illustrated by de Gaulle's tentative *rapprochement* with the Soviet Union in the mid-1960s or French uneasiness about German reunification in the aftermath of the Fall of the Wall in 1989. And French qualms about

---

[30] Frank, 'Le dilemme français', p. 140; Young, 'France's European Policy', pp. 442-48.

American dominance in the world, in recent years demonstrated by France's advocacy of a multipolar world and its resistance to the war against Iraq, are likely to stay with us for some time to come. That being said, continuity does not imply rationality. Ideas, perceptions, identities matter. As mentioned above, obsessive preoccupations sometimes influenced France's German policy. Just as nostalgia and illusions helped shape France's disastrous colonial policy after the war.

Lord Ismay, NATO's first Secretary General, allegedly once stated that NATO's function was "To keep the Russians out, the Americans in, and the Germans down". Like other Europeans, the French were still understandably confused about the new international situation prevailing at the end of the war. But with a few qualifications they could have subscribed to Lord Ismay's statement as early as 1945. At that stage they were slowly realizing that it might be wiser to keep the Russians out rather than to try to drag them in. As far as the Americans and the Germans were concerned, the French needed no convincing that the former should be kept in and the latter down. In addition, some of them were actually pioneers when it came to early attempts at envisioning constructive solutions to the German problem while promoting French economic interests. These ideas would later find their outlet in the process of European integration.

CHAPTER 7

NORDIC DESTINY OR EUROPEAN SOLIDARITY

Scandinavia at a Crossroads after the Second World War

Joachim Lund

Für den Markt nach dem Krieg bedürfe es bei Dänemark nur eines verhältnismäßig kurzen anlaufs. Dänemark stehe gerüstet für die Wirtschaftsprobleme der Nachkriegszeit da.[1]

The German historian Reinhart Koselleck notes that expectations are usually based on the experience of the past. Future and past are closely interrelated.[2] In military theory, it is quite an elementary observation that generals, when they lay out their strategies for the next war, have a tendency to plan for battles of the past. Like military strategy is based on the experiences of previous wars, so it is often the case in political-economic planning. Among Danish political decision-makers in 1939-40, for instance, the response to war and occupation can basically be labeled as an attempt to repeat the Danish foreign policy of the time of the First World War, which had successfully kept the country out of the war and avoided starvation and political chaos. How did Denmark's political establishment handle the outbreak of peace in 1945?

---

[1] Direktor Chr. H. Olesen, chairman of Landsforbundet Dansk Arbejde, *Nachrichte für den Außenhandel*, 19. Mai 1944, Akten Min.-Rat Dr. Breyhan, Bundesarchiv Lichterfelde R2/30.515

[2] For an introduction to Koselleck's *Begriffsgeschichte* see Reinhart Koselleck: *Vergangene Zukunft: Zur Semantik geschichtlicher Zeiten*, Frankfurt am Main, Suhrkamp Verlag 1979.

Did decision-makers try to learn from the past? Did they have any expectations of European co-operation at all? Was there any reason to?

United Press correspondent Howard K. Smith reported from London, Copenhagen and Berlin during the war. Howard K. Smith related directly to the link between the future and the past, when in 1949 he published a book, ambiguously entitled "The State of Europe":

> *It is an astonishing fact, and a tribute to the truth that men do learn, that after this unparalleled disruption [i.e. the Second World War] Europe pulled itself together with remarkable speed and vigor. European wars of the past have invariably been followed by a trail of plagues and famines. But after this, the worst war in Europe's history, there were very few internal upheavals and nothing to match the civil war and the intervention in Russia or the Balkan wars at the end of World War I. No case of mass starvation and no large-scale epidemics occurred. After World War I, it was six heretic years before European economic production attained its prewar levels. After World War II, most of the nations in Europe had recovered prewar industrial levels by the end of 1946, little over a year after the end of hostilities!*

Howard Smith goes on:

> *The reason is clear: men drew on their experience and planned the postwar period. Long before the end of hostilities Bretton Woods formed the basis for economic revival; UNRRA [United Nations Relief and Rehabilitation Administration] pooled all surpluses for distribution to shattered lands according to their needs; international conferences among the Allies laid out makeshift diplomatic **modes de vivre** before the end of the fighting; the UN was formed as an arena for adjusting differences to develop later.*[3]

Howard Smith's account bears the mark of a postwar optimism that hardly existed just a few years earlier, at the liberation of Europe and the end of the war. What kind of Europe was hidden in the ruins in 1945, no one could know. A repetition of the most recent European, prewar past was obviously nothing to strive for. Europe south of Scandinavia was devastated; nationalism and militarism had ruined the hopes of the 1920s of a peaceful and prospering European co-

---

[3] Howard K. Smith: *The State of Europe*. New York: Alfred A. Knopf, 1949, p. 13.

existence. In Scandinavia at this time, it is difficult to find any serious, public debates on how to handle the European question in its postwar chaos. In fact, there was no general concept of Europe in Scandinavia in 1945 at all. This is – at least in part – due to the fact that in Scandinavia,[4] there existed an alternative to European co-operation – *scandinavianism* – which received much more attention at the time. The Scandinavian countries stopped waging war on each other in 1720, and since then they have built a long tradition for co-operation in politics and economy. Until the second half of the 20th century this tradition represented a permanent alternative to a closer engagement in 'European' affairs. It might also explain why the Scandinavian countries have been so reluctant when it comes to European commitments. Therefore, we shall now briefly outline the contours of the scandinavianist tradition before turning to a discussion of the European prospects as seen from Scandinavia in 1945.

Scandinavianism

In Denmark in 1945 there was much talk about Scandinavia or, indeed, the Nordic countries including Finland and Iceland. Solidarity between the Nordic countries had been strengthened during the war. Finland's military alliance with Nazi Germany was regarded as a lesser evil compared to the fact that the Finns were fighting the Soviet Union. Here, the key factor was a general aversion to the Bolshevik regime that had occupied the Baltic States and invaded Finland. At the outbreak of war between Germany and the Soviet Union in 1941, the Danish government had issued an official statement supporting the German attack, and the Danish government had been very close to organizing military support for the Finnish front. A large number of the Danish volunteers for the German SS were driven more by solidarity with Finland than by ideological support to Nazi Germany. Later during the war, Norway received food relief from Denmark and Sweden, which again strengthened the feeling of Nordic solidarity. Sweden, which had upheld its trade with Denmark during the war, provided shelter for thousands of Danish Jews and members of the resistance.

The tradition of Nordic solidarity had its cultural counterpart in the so-called scandinavianism; originally a student's movement rooted in mid-18th century Danish romanticism and nationalism. As Denmark's

---

[4] Contrary to many beliefs, Scandinavia is defined – at least by its inhabitants – as Sweden, Norway and Denmark. In contrast, the Nordic countries ('Norden') also include Iceland and Finland.

role as a European small middleweight power was severely reduced during the Napoleonic Wars, national culture turned inwards and began to look for alternatives to European involvement, and in this situation, closer Scandinavian co-operation provided the answer. The scandinavianist movement suffered a setback when during the Danish-Prussian War in 1864 Sweden refused to side with the Danes. But scandinavianism survived, and books and journals were published under expressive titles, such as the publication by C. Rosenberg, *Political Scandinavism. Hindrances, the Necessity and the Possibilities for its Implementation*.[5] This publication included a proposal for a constitution for a Scandinavian Federation. The success of the Scandinavian monetary union of 1873/75-1914 proved that the movement was not without substance. A shared history, religion, and language proved to be strong features of Denmark, Sweden and Norway. But so did their dependence on economic relations with the world outside the Scandinavian area (see Table 7.1).

Table 7.1

Country	Foreign trade (1936) in £ per capita Export/Import[6]
Denmark	16.0/17.3
Sweden	12.4/10.8
Norway	12.7/15.9
Iceland	29.1/22.4
Finland	8.3/7.4
Germany	5.8/5.1
United Kingdom	9.4/16.1
United States	3.8/3.8

Scandinavianism was invigorated during the First World War – another moment of national crisis – and during the 1930s, when one European democracy after the other had collapsed under the pressure of economic distress, Scandinavian emotions again came to represent a tempting alternative to the harshness of European *Realpolitik*.[7] In March 1940 for instance, when Finland had signed a peace treaty with

---

[5] C. Rosenberg: Den politiske Skandinavisme: *Hindringerne, Nødvendigheden og Muligheden for dens Gjennemførelse: Med Forslag til en skandinavisk Forbundsforfatning*. Særtryk af Dansk Maanedsskrift, København 1864. See also Henrik Becker-Christensen: *Skandinaviske drømme og politiske realiteter: den politiske skandinavisme i Danmark 1830-1850*, Århus 1981.

[6] Molin, Nissen, Skodvin, Soikkanen and Weibull: *Norden under 2. Verdenskrig*, Copenhagen 1979, p. 28.

[7] Again in 1925, Norwegian author Gunnar Gunnarsson had proposed a Nordic Union, though without much support at the time.

Nordic Destiny or European Solidarity?

the Soviet Union, there was a serious attempt at establishing a Nordic defense league between Sweden, Norway and Finland, which was only cancelled when Moscow declared it to be a threat to the Finno-Soviet treaty. During the German occupation of Denmark and Norway, scandinavianism again came to the forefront, linking up with the need of the population to distance itself from Nazism and German imperialism. The conflict between those who promoted a closer relationship with Germany and those who advocated the alternative of Scandinavian co-operation even found its way to Danish business life, where groupings like the Institute for Economic Issues and the Study Group of 1940 would enthusiastically investigate the possibilities within the German *Grossraumwirtschaft*, while the association Dansk Arbejde committed itself to the Scandinavian cause. Even in June 1941, at the height of German power in Europe, the association claimed that contrary to what the official German propaganda said, Denmark would be better off pursuing a higher degree of autarchy and a closer Nordic co-operation. The German legation in Copenhagen rightly considered this attitude to be a result of "certain Scandinavian efforts".[8]

In Sweden, where national interests could be debated in the open during the war, scandinavianism gained momentum in 1942/43. Foreign Minister Rickard Sandler had already pleaded for a much closer Nordic co-operation, and now a group of leading public figures published a pamphlet with the title *The United States of the Nordic Countries*, which was translated into Danish and Finnish and attracted widespread attention.[9] The discussion continued across the Swedish-Danish border during 1943. But there were also voices that warned against Scandinavian optimism: Swedish historian Herbert Tingsten wrote that much of the debate about Nordic postwar co-operation was based on illusions and wishful thinking, and pointed out that Scandinavia would not be strong enough to face military challenges and that it would be necessary for the Nordic countries to look for security in a broader, international organization. This is what compelled the leading Danish Social Democrat, Hartvig Frisch, to write – in 1944 – that Swedish neutrality would be crucial in the future and that a Nordic peace league must not isolate itself but would have to be connected with what he called "international peace politics".[10] Five years later, in 1949, the

---

[8] Head of German legation in Copenhagen Cecil von Renthe-Fink to Auswärtiges Amt, 11.6.1941. Bundesarchiv Lichterfelde R 901, 68049.

[9] Karl Petander, Anders Örne, W. Kleen: *Nordens förente Stater*, 1942.

[10] Hartvig Frisch: *Tænkt og talt under Krigen*. København: Fremad, 1945, p. 118.

Danish lawyer K.A. Wieth-Knudsen published a pamphlet addressing this new phenomenon, which he called Atlantic Scandinavianism.[11]

After the war, with the emergence of the Cold War, scandinavianism was indeed more or less dissolved. A last attempt to unite Scandinavia was seen in 1948/49, when the governments of Sweden, Norway and Denmark entered into negotiations concerning a Scandinavian defense league. But with Denmark and Norway deciding to sign the North Atlantic Treaty Organization in 1949 and Sweden holding on to neutrality, time had run out. Since then, Nordic co-operation has been reduced to the establishment of the Nordic Council in 1952 and a Nordic passport union, while the EFTA (European Free Trade Association) provided the basis for economic co-operation between Nordic and other small states on the fringe of the EEC.[12]

Economic Planning for Postwar Scandinavia

In economic theory, Koselleck's concept of the linkage between future and the past may be placed within an institutional framework via the concept of 'path dependence'.[13] The idea is that actions and decisions taken in the past restrain possible choices in the future. In Scandinavia, this meant that the different role these countries had always played in the northern periphery of 'the real Europe' could not be abandoned overnight. Indeed, the Nordic countries were no obvious candidates for the EEC when it was established during the 1950s. The point was spelled out when the first president of the European Economic Commission, Dr. Walter Hallstein, in a speech in 1961 stated that "the area covered by the Communities is identical with the territory of those States which were brought to the edge of physical and political destruction by the wanton national-socialist adventure. This experiment has left in the hearts of these nations the fervent wish that such a thing shall never happen again."[14] Hallstein was obviously forgetting what the peoples of Norway and Denmark remembered quite clearly: that those countries had in fact also belonged to the occupied countries during the war – not to mention East and Southeast Europe.

---

[11] K.A. Wieth-Knudsen: *Atlanterhavs-Skandinavisme? Danmark på skillevejen*, København 1949.
[12] See Lars Hovbakke Sørensen: *Nordenforestillinger i dansk politik 1945-1968*, Århus 2005.
[13] See Douglas North: *Institutions, Institutional Change and Economic Performance*, New York, Cambridge University Press 1990.
[14] Cit. E. Strauss: *European Reckoning. The Six and Britain's Future*, London: George Allen & Unwin ltd. 1962, p. 13.

Economy and security very much dominated the discussion about Scandinavia's future role in a European context. As mentioned earlier, the Nordic security problem was settled in 1949. Economically, the process of leaving the idea of closer Scandinavian co-operation has been much longer and much more painful – although today it seems to be working quite well and nearing its completion. Established in 1960, the purpose of the EFTA was to provide shelter and opportunities for those democratic European countries that for one reason or another had not joined the European Club. But the organization was undermined as the UK and Denmark left in 1970 to join the EEC three years later, while Sweden and Finland joined the EU in 1995, leaving Norway and Iceland as the only remaining Nordic countries in EFTA.

Path dependence was very much at work when it came to Scandinavian economic postwar expectations of Europe. After May 1945, Scandinavia had to find its way into new trade patterns defined by the growing split between East and West and a reorientation towards the international market economy. The wartime experience – first of all the fear of again being denied access to foreign supplies – put its mark on the politics of postwar Scandinavia. But whereas other Western European societies at the same time struggled to reinstall parliamentarian democracy as a legitimate régime and overcome the crisis of political parties, Scandinavia already enjoyed a high degree of democratic consensus, which stemmed from the significant political agreements that had formed part of parliamentarian daily life during the 1930s and had kept the totalitarian movements at bay. This remarkable achievement of political institutions in the prewar years was of crucial importance for Scandinavia's political culture after 1945. Political parties had developed into powerful interest groups, which represented almost every part of the population, with at strong commitment to parliamentarian democracy, and able to form and keep stable coalition governments. In all three countries, the governments of the 1930s consisted of Social Democrats in coalition with the party representing the large group of small farmers; in Denmark since 1929, in Norway since 1935, in Sweden since 1932 (Social Democrats alone), and since 1935 (in coalition with the farmers' party). At the same time, these coalition governments were forced to allow the opposition to have some influence on crisis management, something that would, in the long run, win over most of those who had questioned democracy's ability to cope with large-scale economic crisis. In both Sweden and Denmark, this tendency became manifest with the national compromises of 1933, when decisive agreements between the governments and the liberal big farmers' parties were reached, clearing the path to social reform, job creation and support for the farmers. Symbolically, the national Danish agreement was reached on January 31, 1933, on the very day of Germany's decisive step towards dictatorship. When Denmark's democracy was put to the test following Germany's occupation in April 1940, the democratic opposition parties were included in the government, which now represented 95% of the population and remained in office with minor changes until August 1943. In Sweden, from late 1939 the coalition consisted of all major political parties and lasted throughout the war. Norway's democracy was put on hold as a result of its war with Germany. However, in Norway, as in Sweden and Denmark, the democratic political culture itself proved to be strong enough to resist the repeated attacks from German authorities and the local fascist movement.

A number of other stabilizing institutions characterized the Scandinavian countries in 1945, which made them differ even more from their fellow European countries. Unions and employers' organizations dominated and regulated the labour market through a voluntary system of negotiated compromises. Unlike Belgium, France and Greece, social stability and cultural homogeneity made revolutionary changes unwanted by an overwhelming majority of the population. Unlike Belgium, Czechoslovakia and Yugoslavia, there were no serious nationality or language problems; and unlike the Netherlands and Germany, there were no serious religious divides.[15]

Moreover, the economic structure of the three countries was essentially intact in 1945. If we turn to Danish industry, we find a widespread optimism as the war drew to a close. In 1940, industry had surpassed agriculture as the country's largest economic sector, and despite a disturbing lack of raw materials and a pressing need for new investments and modernization, industrial production had increased even during the war. Now, according to the director of the national bank, the ultimate goal was to promote further industrial growth.[16]

Although gifted with such kinds of 'competitive advantage', five years at the mercy of Nazi Germany seriously hampered Scandinavia's

---

[15] To readers of Scandinavian languages, an excellent introduction to the theme is to be found in Molin et al, 1979. See also Henrik S. Nissen (ed.): *Scandinavia during the Second World War*, Minneapolis 1983, and Patrick Salmon: *Scandinavia and the Great Powers 1890-1940*, Cambridge 1997.

[16] Phil Giltner: 'The Success of Collaboration: Denmark's Self-Assessment of its Economic Position after Five Years of Nazi Occupation', *Journal of Contemporary History* 36 (2001), no. 3, pp. 485-506 (500-501).

ability to recover, because of those countries' immense dependence on foreign supplies and international trade. In 1945, as in 1940, the major trading partners changed places. Apart from that, nothing had changed fundamentally since the inter-war years.

In 1945, Scandinavia rejoined the global market of which it had been a part before Nazi Germany closed continental Europe from the world in 1939/1940. At the outbreak of war in 1939, the three Scandinavian countries were among the economically most dependent countries in the world, and although the war had very different impacts on Norway, Denmark, and non-occupied Sweden, economically, the three countries had very much shared the experience of small, politically neutral and economically advanced countries with an extraordinary dependence on foreign trade. Between the world wars, through a complicated trade system of imports and exports clearing, the Scandinavian countries compensated for their lack of many natural resources. This foreign dependence determined their policy of adaptation towards Germany during the Second World War – although it must be said that the Norwegian society as a *Reichskommissariat* experienced a much greater German political pressure than the two others; during the war, the two sovereign states of Denmark and Sweden actually had much more in common in the political-economic sphere than is usually assumed.[17] In short, between 1940 and 1945, Germany's eagerness to exploit the resources of the Scandinavian countries went hand in hand with a local willingness to co-operate with the Germans, rescuing the small Scandinavian countries from relapsing into pre-modern, de-industrialized societies.

From the outset in 1945 it was fairly clear that the major foreign markets of Denmark, Norway and Sweden were to be found outside Scandinavia. Due to a serious shortage of almost every kind of imported raw material during the war, industrial and agricultural production had decreased. In 1945, the need for opening old channels of im-

---

[17] Martin Fritz: 'Swedish Adaptation to German Domination in the Second World War'; Joachim Lund: 'Business Elite Networks in Denmark: Adjusting to German Domination'; both in: Joachim Lund (ed.): *Working for the New Order. European Business under German Domination 1939-1945*, Copenhagen: CBS Press 2006, pp. 129-39 and 115-28; Alan S. Milward: *The Fascist Economy in Norway*, Oxford 1972; Robert Bohn: *Reichskommissariat Norwegen. "Nationalsozialistische Neuordnung" und Kriegswirtschaft*, München 2000; Hans-Erich Volkmann: *Ökonomie und Expansion. Grundzüge der NS-Wirtschaftspolitik*, hrsg. von Bernhard Chiari, München 2003, pp. 36-41; Klaus Wittmann: *Schwedens Wirtschaftsbeziehungen zum Dritten Reich 1933-1945*. Studien zur modernen Geschichte 23, München/Wien 1978.

port was evident, as was the need to secure the exports necessary to finance those supplies. What were the expectations of Scandinavian economic experts to the postwar development? What were the chances of re-establishing Scandinavia's prewar global trade connections in order to facilitate economic growth and social recovery?

In the eyes of Scandinavian economists, the chances of securing Scandinavia's trade connections and promoting economic growth were European and global, not Scandinavian. In 1943-45, western politicians and economists began to look into a future world that would not be dominated by Germany. Different German attempts to rethink the European plans and propaganda, such as the *Europäische Wirtschaftsplanung of the Reichsministerium für Rüstung und Kriegsproduktion* or the propaganda stemming from the *Europa-Ausschuss* of the *Auswärtiges Amt* in 1942-43,[18] were largely ignored. But also British and American economic planning for the postwar period had begun at an early stage of the war. Experts had pointed to the fact that during the First World War, the winning side had failed to produce a plan for economic reconstruction, making a lasting peace impossible. Already in 1919, the famous British economist John Maynard Keynes had dealt with the question in his *Economic Consequences of the Peace*. Winning the war was not enough; one had to win the peace too. Inspired by Keynes, in his *Economic Consequences of the Second World War* from 1941, economic advisor to the International Labour Office and later advisor to the first US delegation to the United Nations, Lewis L. Lorwin, called for "A World New Deal".[19]

Getting accurate information on what came from the other side was not an easy job, especially in Denmark and Norway, but words of Allied plans began to reach Scandinavia, and gradually, more became known about the Keynes-plan regarding a transnational monetary authority, the British Beveridge-plan of June 1942 on social security, and the American White-plan, which founded the basis of the Bretton Woods-agreements in the summer of 1944.[20]

---

[18] Hans Werner Neulen: 'Deutsche Besatzungspolitik in Westeuropa – zwischen Unterdrückung und Kollaboration', in: Karl Dietrich Bracher et al: *Deutschland 1933-1945: Neue Studien zur nationalsozialistischen Herrschaft*, 2. Aufl. Bonner Schriften zur Politik und Zeitgeschichte 23, Düsseldorf 1993, pp. 404-25 (416-17).
[19] Lewis L. Lorwin: *Det andra världkrigets economiska följder*, Stockholm 1942 (Swedish ed.), esp. foreword and pp. 461-78.
[20] 'Internationale Valutaplaner for Efterkrigstiden, 1. Del', *Tidsskrift for Industri* 17, 1. september 1943; 'Internationale Valutaplaner for Efterkrigstiden, 2. Del', *Tidsskrift for Industri* 19, 10. oktober 1943; Giltner 2001, p. 503.

Nordic Destiny or European Solidarity?

In Scandinavia, political regulation of the economy as a means of equalizing business cycles was already a tested tool. In January 1943, in Denmark the Ministry of Finance established the so-called 'Professors' Committee' with the double purpose of fighting the immediate danger of inflation and forestalling the economic problems that might occur following a German defeat and the breakdown of the continental European *Grossraumwirtschaft*. Because of the problem of the so-called idle money, and an even greater projected shortage of consumer goods, raw materials, and fuels as an immediate result of a German collapse, the primary task of the committee was to provide means to control the expected inflation and its damages on the economy.

In Sweden, also in spring 1943, a large number of political institutions, economic agencies and trade unions began analyzing aspects of postwar planning. One initial observation was that unemployment would rise because of demobilisation and forestry workers who would lose their jobs when imports of coal and oil recommenced and replaced wood as a source of fuel. Like in Denmark, the job situation was at the core of the analyses. In February 1944, the Swedish 'Committee for Economic Post War Planning' was established in order to evaluate the findings of the different research institutions and make political propositions to cope with the economic problems in sight. Gunnar Myrdal from the celebrated 'Stockholm School', Social Democrat, post-war Secretary of Trade, and Scandinavia's leading Keynesian economist, chaired the committee which is usually referred to as the 'Myrdal Commission'. It eventually produced 12 volumes, the last one in November 1945. Already in 1944, Myrdal had published his book *Varning för fredsoptimism* (*Warning Against Peace Optimism*), in which he predicted a world crisis after the war, beginning in the US.[21] The previous year, in a review of Lewis Lorwins book on the economic consequences of the Second World War, Gunnar Myrdal had called for international planning and control of the world economy in order to avoid wars and revolutions which would produce future economic chaos.[22]

Alongside the work being prepared in official political institutions, trade unions and political parties also made their own analyses. In 1945, the Danish Social Democrats published a comprehensive party programme for *Future Denmark*, authored by Jens Otto Krag, econo-

---

[21] For a thorough analysis of Gunnar Myrdal's early work, see Örjan Appelqvist: *Bruten brygga. Gunnar Myrdal och Sveriges ekonomiska efterkrigspolitik 1943-1947*, Stockholm 2000.
[22] Appelqvist (2000), p. 47.

103

mist, later prime minister, and author of the study *War Economy and Postwar Problems*, which was published in 1944.[23] In an effort to catch up with the prospering communist party, the programme was heavy with socialist rhetoric and a vast socialisation programme. During the war, Swedish Social Democrats had passed on Keynesian economics to occupied Denmark.[24]

In Sweden the Social Democratic government remained in power after 1945, and in comparison with Denmark, Keynesian economics is considered to have been even more profound. It has even been stated that for a long time Sweden was actually the only country to pursue a policy of Keynesianism, long before Keynes.[25] In 1944, Sweden's Labour Movement issued a programme that anticipated a postwar depression and was somewhat more pessimistic than the Danish one. In Norway, where political institutions had been crushed during the occupation, the work undertaken by the illegal political parties, the underground movement, and the exiled government in London was the most important. The most significant result was the joint declaration of the four big political parties, drafted in autumn 1944 and officially approved in June 1945 as the foundation of postwar reconstruction of the Norwegian society.

Turning to the work of the Danish Professors' Committee and the Swedish Myrdal Commission, it is interesting to note that when it came to expectations of the reconstruction of trade patterns, the Danish and Swedish investigations pointed in quite different directions. Both parties feared a collapse in international trade, but with opposite effects. The Swedish Myrdal Commission expected a quick recovery followed by a long-term depression with deflation and unemployment, due to decreasing international demand.[26] Danish (and Norwegian) analyses feared the opposite: as a result of the occupation and exorbitant selling prices on the German and *Wehrmacht* market, Denmark

---

[23] Niels Wium Olesen: *Jens Otto Krag. En socialdemokratisk politiker. De unge år 1914-1950*. Esbjerg 2002, pp. 207-78.

[24] Niels Wium Olesen: 'Jens Otto Krag og Keynes', *Arbejderhistorie* 1, 2001, pp. 38-60; Olesen (2002), p. 213, 219-21.

[25] Cay Sévon: *Visionen om Europa. Svensk neutralitet och europeisk återuppbyggnad 1945-1948*, Helsinki 1995, pp. 31-32.

[26] The Swedish predicaments corresponded to the contemporary American forecasts for the postwar period which, inspired by Keynes and with the well-known economist Alvin Hansen in front, pleaded for large anti-unemployment measures. See Sven Ulrich Palme: 'Politics and Economic Theory in Allied Planning for Peace, 1944-1945', *The Scandinavian Economic History Review* Vol. VII, no 1 (1959), pp. 67-78.

and Norway had experienced an involuntary, large-scale abundance of money, and demands on non-existent goods constituted a permanent risk of inflation. In each of the three countries, the gloomy predictions were proven wrong; in Sweden from 1946, inflation, not deflation, set the agenda – which came as something of a surprise to economic analysts.[27] In Denmark and Norway, inflation was kept within limits. In the Danish case this was a result of the implementation of the Keynesian politics, which economic experts recommended so strongly in order to prevent a crisis. The currency reform of 1945 swallowed much of the 'idle money', and a one-off tax in 1946 secured yet another part. In Norway, in contrast, the government hesitated to apply such drastic measures; instead, inland debt, caused by the Germans, was paid largely by Marshall help.[28]

With the risk of overstating the argument, Danish disappointment and Swedish relief might perhaps fit a general description of the immediate postwar years' foreign trade development of the two countries. But what was the reason for the serious discrepancy between the conclusions reached by the Swedish Myrdal Commission and the Danish Professors' Committee? The answer may seem obvious: More than being just a technical discussion about crisis of demand versus crisis of supply, the core of the difference of opinion was the very politicized question of whether to fight inflation or limit unemployment, and the discrepancies were based on differences in fundamental political views. Questions on the future of Europe were very much intertwined with the analysis of economic issues, and as overriding political and ideological questions on the future economic direction of Scandinavian societies were put on the agenda, there was no such thing as neutrality. The Social Democrat Gunnar Myrdal, in his advocacy for "organized, free trade", also favoured the struggle against social inequality. In wartime Sweden, the Social Democrats were at the height of their power and decided exclusively which kind of experts were to lead the way into the postwar era. Swedish governmental economic planning thus became almost identical with the party programme of the Social Democrats. In contrast, perhaps the most prominent member of the Danish Professors' Committee, Thorkil Kristensen, was a liberal economist with a basic taste for liberalisation of trade as a means of maximising the competitiveness of industry and agriculture. During the war, the Danish Social Democratic government leaders, in a permanent defen-

---

[27] Sten Carlson: *Svensk historia* vol. 2, 3rd ed. Stockholm 1970, p. 589; Lars Magnusson: *Sveriges ekonomiska historia*, Stockholm 1997, p. 410.
[28] Giltner (2001), p. 490.

sive position due to the German occupation, had to pay their dues to conservative and liberal coalition partners; more than the Myrdal Commission, the composition of the Professors' Committee, headed by a senior civil servant, reflected the political balance of the coalition government, making room for liberal economists like Thorkil Kristensen. The latter became minister of finance in the liberal government of 1945-47.

To be sure, the conclusions of the Professors' Committee were not undisputed. Colleagues found them somewhat misplaced and warned that the measures of fiscal policy restrictions the committee recommended would increase unemployment.[29] Far from all of the committee's suggestions were implemented. But as a whole, Danish governmental economic planning for the postwar era came to symbolize the compromise of government policy of occupied Denmark. Perhaps this historical background is the reason why Danish postwar predictions seem more balanced. Just like the wartime coalition government represented a compromise between Socialist, liberal and conservative interests, so did the findings of the Professors' Committee.

However, political differences are not sufficient when it comes to explaining discrepancies in economic analyses. Here, too, one should not disregard the presence of a certain amount of path dependency. Denmark was occupied and had for years tried to tackle the problem of inflation caused by 'the idle money'. With good reason, the experts of the Professors' Committee were nervous about what would happen if and when the German economy collapsed and there would be even fewer products available for the Danish consumer. Sweden, on the other hand, had remained independent during the war and had other experiences. Here, unlike Denmark, wages had been allowed to follow the prices, but rising wage and price levels had been limited thanks to efficient government control. Since no extra billions of Swedish *kronor* had been poured into society, inflation had been insignificant. Instead, Sweden looked to the conclusion of the First World War to get an idea of what might come from the conclusion of the Second.[30] With this historical perspective in mind, Myrdal and other leading Swedish economists had little doubt that a serious setback in the international economy was to be expected. In their writings, while promoting the

---

[29] Per H. Hansen: 'Dansk økonomi under besættelsen: Ved vi nok?' *Den jyske Historiker* 73, 1996, pp. 33-54 (54).
[30] I make no claim of being the first to make this observation. See e.g. Sévon (1995), p. 31.

idea of free trade, they also left room for the option of reverting to prewar protectionism, autarchy and a resulting global market contraction.

Fortunately, such economic detours never became necessary. After the war, Sweden, having experienced a steady economic growth since 1942-43, profited well from the shortages of basic industrial commodities in other European countries, and the expected lack of demand did not occur. Employment remained high, and economists could turn to the more pressing problem of limiting inflation.[31] Moreover, the situation called for – and to some extent resulted in – an extensive reorganization of Sweden's industrial production, which to a large extent had been directed towards the home and German markets. By the outbreak of the Korean War, iron ore, steel, wooden articles, paper and pulp constituted almost 70% of the country's exports and by 1951, the country's terms of trade had improved by 50% since 1945.[32] On the import side, the sudden growth that followed the outbreak of peace in 1945 somewhat overwhelmed the country. The following year, a huge foreign trade deficit had occurred with a serious impact on national gold reserves and foreign currency. Gunnar Myrdal, now minister of trade, warned that import regulations might become necessary, and in March 1947, a direct, general import prohibition was issued. Finally in 1949, the Swedish *krona*, which in 1946 had been revaluated by 17%, followed a range of other countries (among them Denmark and Norway) and was now devaluated by 30%. Inflation grew even faster after the outbreak of the Korean War, enhancing the need for political stability and causing the Social Democrats to give up their monopoly of power in 1951 and form a coalition with the agrarian liberals, which would last until 1957.[33]

In Scandinavia, the outbreak of the Korean War in 1950 set off a wave of anti-inflationist policy. Another factor was the Marshall Plan. But long before the three countries approved Marshall Aid, they had tried to make their way back to the global market, and measures were taken in order to secure the foreign currency necessary for the most basic imports. We shall now see, how, in Denmark's case, this operation was synonymous with an almost feverish attempt to reconstruct the pre-war pattern of agricultural exports, which still made up ¾ of the country's foreign currency income.

---

[31] Ebba Dohlman: *National Welfare and Economic Interdependence. The Case of Sweden's Foreign Trade Policy*, Oxford 1989, pp. 65-69.
[32] Lennart Petersson: *Svensk utrikeshandel 1871-1980. En studie i den intraindustrielle handelns framväxt*. Lund Economic Studies 30, Malmö 1984, pp. 142-43.
[33] Magnusson (1997), pp. 411 f.; Appelqvist (2000), p. 21.

Danish Bacon Goes West (Again)

If there was one concept of Europe in Denmark in 1945, it was an economic one. The big question was, if the country would be able to re-establish pre-war trading patterns and to divert its agricultural export to the UK just as quickly and easily as the reorientation to the German market had been in 1940.[34] Denmark's re-entry into the global market economy would take place within a European trade "system", which was being reconstructed the way it had functioned in the 1930s, with bilateral agreements and extensive imports and foreign currency controls. In Europe, during the first years after 1945, "What was talked about was often grand in conception, payments unions, free-trade areas, customs unions and economic unions, replacing the harsh facts of the 1940s with the progressive dreams of the 1850s. What was done, in contrast, remained petty."[35] In fact, by the end of 1947, a greater proportion of Western Europe's trade was conducted in this way than it had been in the 1930s.[36]

In Denmark, the liberal government of 1945-47 defined reconstruction politics as making sure that agriculture remained the dominant factor in the Danish economy, whereas the Social Democratic government of 1947-50 emphasised the need for further industrialisation. Certainly, there was a need in 1945 to improve conditions of agriculture, which during the war had been subject to overexhaustion and short-term priorities. But due to a fast growing foreign exchange deficit, the necessary imports of fodder could only be limited, and in the first postwar years, the quantities of fodder available were still not sufficient to boost agricultural production. Such economic problems were eventually to promote Denmark's approval of the Marshall Plan in autumn 1947/spring 1948. Under the American aid programme, until 1953, Denmark would receive 1,7 bill. DKK, which would cover roughly 50% of the country's dollar import in 1949-51, finance raw materials for agriculture, renew production facilities – and curtail Communist agitation. It was well into the 1950s, before parts of the

---

[34] For en evaluation of Denmark's reorientation towards the western hemisphere, see e.g. Hans Branner: 'Options and Goals in Danish European Policy since 1945: Explaining Small State Behaviour and Foreign Policy Change', in: Hans Branner/Morten Kelstrup (eds.): *Denmark's Policy towards Europe after 1945: History, Theory and Options*, Odense 2000, pp. 333-80.
[35] Milward (1984), p. 227
[36] Ibid., p. 220.

Marshall funds could be used efficiently to better conditions of industry and promote industrial exports.[37]

In 1945, long before the industrial effects of the Marshall Aid and the OEEC (Organization for European Economic Cooperation) which accompanied it, agricultural exports still relied heavily on the crumbling German market and the necessity to find its way back to the British. And as occupied Germany gradually became self-sufficient in foodstuffs, the British market became even more important.[38]

The breakthrough came in July 1946, when British and the Danish negotiators reached a trade agreement with a term of three years and somewhat better prices on bacon, butter and eggs than expected on the side of the Danes. However, higher import prices and wages soon consumed the higher export prices. At the same time, the Danish secretary of trade had cancelled restrictions on imports from the UK in an attempt to comply with domestic pressure of liberalizing trade. The result was, of course, the opposite: rationing and import limitations continued – actually reducing imports by 10% in 1947-48 – and a whole new ministry of supplies had to be established. Official statistics show a Danish foreign trade surplus of 206 million DKK in 1945, transforming into a disastrous deficit of 1.231 million DKK the following year, with an improved result in 1947 of 780 million DKK.

In February 1948, the trade agreement with the UK was renewed, again with favourable Danish export prices, and from that year, the Marshall Aid began to have an effect on the country's import abilities. But the devaluation of the pound by 30% in September 1949 produced another setback in the development of Danish foreign economic relations. Denmark along with 16 other countries followed the pound, the Danish devaluation of 44% making imports of grain and other fodder all the more expensive. Again, imports of consumer goods had to be reduced in order to secure the import of raw materials for the foreign exchange earning agriculture. American protectionism, the Berlin blockade, the economic boycott of Eastern Europe, and a growing pressure for liberalisation of trade from the part of the OEEC charac-

---

[37] An introduction is given in: Vibeke Sørensen: 'Fra Marshall-plan til de store markedsdannelser, 1945-59', in: Johnny Laursen et al: *Danmark i Europa 1945-93*, Copenhagen 1994, pp. 9-91. See also Vibeke Sørensen: *Denmark's Social Democratic Government & the Marshall Plan, 1947-1950* (ed. Mogens Rüdiger), Copenhagen 2001.

[38] Danish-British relations in the first postwar years are treated in Rasmus Mariager: *"I tillid og varm sympati"* ["In Confidence and Warm Sympathy"], Copenhagen 2006.

terised the years 1949-50. In spring 1950, the central clearing of the EPU (European Payments Union) replaced all bilateral trade agreements within the OEEC area, and in May, the Schuman Plan concerning a closer European integration was issued.

In Denmark, rationing of coal, coke, rice and chocolate was lifted in spring, symbolizing the slow but steady improvement in the economic situation. But in June, the Korean War broke out, and again, the recovery of the Danish foreign trade experienced a setback as supplies were threatened and prices skyrocketed. In fact, Danish decision-makers must have felt the outbreak of war was something of a *September 1939 revisited*. The price situation forced the government to issue a set of new import restrictions, which would save 300 million DKK in foreign exchange, far from enough to stop the foreign exchange deficit from rising again, reaching 500 million DKK at the end of the year. Parliamentary opposition to the proposed restrictions was heavy, and when the expected lifting of the rationing of sugar, coffee and butter had to be abandoned, there was enough indignation within the political opposition to provoke new elections. Held in September, they allowed the Social Democratic government to stay in power, but only for another six weeks. In October 1950, a new liberal government was formed, after the Social Democrats lost a parliamentary vote on the lifting of butter rationing.

Table 7.2[39]

Table 7.3[40]

Year/Country	Distribution of Denmark's Exports 1935-1950 (mill. DKK)		Distribution of Denmark's Imports 1935-1950 (mill. DKK)	
	(West) Germany	United Kingdom	West Germany	United Kingdom
1935	203	731	292	479
1936	278	742	376	542
1937	296	823	407	642
1938	304	861	399	562
1939	369	827	470	573
1940	1089	190	770	150
1941	977		1021	1
1942	693		848	
1943	990		869	
1944	1090		908	
1945	183	310	159	107
1946	73	514	118	1289
1947	34	627	92	671
1948	39	831	119	889
1949	232	1564	106	1339
1950	787	1931	571	1869

---

[39] Hans Chr. Johansen: *Dansk historisk statistik 1814-1980*, Copenhagen 1985, pp. 209-10.

[40] Ibid. pp. 214-15.

Only in the mid-1950s was Denmark able to lift the last rationing and gradually leave the system of regulation of foreign economic relations, which had been introduced in 1932. As a small state whose economic development was closely connected to that of its trading partners, Denmark could do – and did – very little in order to promote the liberalisation of international trade. The country succeeded in returning to the old relationship with the UK (see Tables 7.2 and 7.3), and as Denmark's dependence on the UK grew, the country followed its most important trading partner down to their simultaneous admission to the EEC in 1973. Although Germany today is Denmark's most important trading partner, Denmark's reluctance to accept the abolition of the Danish currency in favour of the Euro has been closely connected to the British retaining the pound.

Today, Denmark's loyalties are split between Great Britain, "Europe" (meaning the EU) and the nationalistic idea of selfsufficiency. Scandinavia is but than a geographic notion – and a historical experience.

CHAPTER 8

GERMAN WRITERS' ATTITUDE TOWARDS EUROPE IN THE FIRST POSTWAR YEARS

Per Øhrgaard

One of the bigger surprises in German literary life at the end of the Second World War was the so-called "empty cupboards", the lack of manuscripts describing life in Germany during the Nazi regime and the years of war.[1] Of course, paper restrictions and allied censorship put a limit on the publication of German literature – and foreign literature as well for that matter – but even when the ban was finally lifted not much was discovered, neither poetry nor fiction nor diaries,[2] especially not much written by members of the younger generation. There are reasons for this: First, you might say that people had been busy with other things than writing poetry or novels, and that the muses are silent in times of war, but this is only part of the explanation. Most of the young men had been at the front far away from home, and the women had had enough to do with keeping up with the increasing difficulties in daily life, among them the bombings of German cities. Furthermore, manuscripts might have been lost in the fires following the bombs, and finally literature written in the times of despotism might indeed have "lost value" after the German surrender. What could have been of interest in, say, 1941, would perhaps seem obsolete in 1945. The first literary works to be published in Germany after May 1945 were with a

---

[1] This contribution is part of a work in progress dealing with the "Europeanization" of German intellectuals after 1945. A shorter version was presented at the Tenth International Congress of the IVG (Internationale Vereinigung der Germanisten) in Paris, August 2005. Much has, of course, already been written on this subject; but this is not the place for a bibliography.

[2] At least not in the first postwar years; later quite a few witness reports were published, as late as in the 90'es the breathtaking diary of Viktor Klemperer, *Ich will Zeugnis ablegen bis zum letzten. Tagebücher 1933-1945,* Berlin 1995.

few exceptions works of the older generation of writers – provided that they were not prohibited from publishing because of their affiliation with the Nazi regime. Many years later Heinrich Böll said in an interview: Today no one easily imagines how difficult it was to write only half a page of prose in 1945.[3]

The Third Reich lasted for only twelve years, but in terms of culture – and thus literature – it neither started in 1933, nor did it disappear in 1945. The genuine party or propaganda literature was, of course, gone; but the Nazis had not invented their cultural policy from scratch; they had integrated and exploited currents that had for a long time been strong and that lived on after the war. In a certain sense the cultural policy of the GDR – *sans comparaison!* – was more restrictive than that of the Nazis, simply because the communist ideology never did appeal to a majority of Germans, whereas the uneasiness with modernity and the longing for "blood and soil" were widespread – and this not only in Germany. Furthermore one has to keep in mind that it was much easier for the authorities in the thirties to cut off a country than it would be today: neither media nor tourism was very developed yet, so the regime only had to cut a rather small number of connections in order to keep Germany isolated. Even so, the Germans did not necessarily feel isolated at all: during the Olympic Games of Berlin in 1936 they might even consider Germany the centre of the world.

Thus, to catch up with Western or rather European cultural life in 1945 was not just a matter of opening the borders – let alone the fact that they were not opened until several years later; foreigners visited Germany, some – although few – emigrants came back, but only very few Germans were allowed to travel abroad. So, what did international culture mean to the Germans of 1945, what did the notion of "Europe" mean? And how international were, after all, those Germans who claimed to speak for the young generation and to articulate its commitment to Europe and not just to the rebuilding of Germany itself? In the following remarks I shall concentrate on the periodical *Der Ruf* (The Call) which became the nucleus of the later so-called "Group 47", the most influential association of West German writers after 1945, although is was in fact no association, but only came into existence once or twice a year when its "members" met.

The story of the Group 47 is a matter of its own and not to be told here.[4] First a few remarks on the cultural policy of the Allied forces.

---

[3] Cf. *Die Gruppe 47. Bericht. Kritik. Polemik.* Ein Handbuch herausgegeben von Reinhard Lettau. Neuwied u. Berlin 1967, p. 334.

[4] See Heinz Ludwig Arnold, *Die Gruppe 47*, Reinbek 2004 (with bibliography).

Each occupation authority controlled, of course, its own part of Germany, and each had developed plans for the implementation of some kind of re-education, although only the Americans would name it this way. For the Soviets, Stalin had already told Milovan Djilas that in present and future wars the victor would not only occupy a territory but also install his own political, economic and social system, and that was the way it went in the Soviet zone of Germany – which, by the way, at first seemed attractive to quite a few literary emigrants (and later also to some who had first tried to get a foothold in the West like Stephan Hermlin, Hans Mayer or Bertolt Brecht). At the beginning the powers did co-operate: Americans and Soviets exchanged e.g. lists of books to be removed from the libraries, and as far as books sent to Germany to educate the Germans are concerned there is the well-known episode concerning George Orwell's *Animal Farm*: First, the U.S. authorities did not want the novel to go to Germany in order not to offend the Soviet allies, but later the novel was spread all over West Germany in a large number of copies in order to warn the Germans against totalitarianism. The French, who finally got their own occupation zone, obsessed with the threat from a Germany that had three times in seventy years invaded France, pursued a very severe occupation policy but at the same time conducted a very active cultural policy that paid off in the long run and laid the ground for the later reconciliation between the two countries. The British, too, had made up plans for the renovation of German culture. Let us not abstain from quoting from a very British list of issues and themes that should be kept away from – or on the contrary forced upon – the Germans. Under "theology" the British expert suggests: "Leave that to the German clergy" – and under "philosophy" one finds a nice laconic prescription: "Best to give it a rest."[5]

So what then was introduced in Germany, and what did the Germans themselves reach out for? In most cases works that expressed or seemed to express the same feelings and attitudes that prevailed in Germany itself. Ernest Hemingway or Jean Anouilh, Thornton Wilder or Jean-Paul Sartre were above all regarded as typical of the time, rather than typical of one country or the other. The experience of war, of destruction of all values, of disillusion, was common to all, and thus the common suffering of the war seemed to be the first step back to

---

[5] Rhys W. Williams: "'The Selections of the Committee are not in Accordance with the Requirements of Germany': Selected Book Scheme in the British Zone of Germany" (1945-1950), in: Alan Bance (ed.), *The Cultural Legacy of the British Occupation in Germany. The London Symposium,* Stuttgart 1997, p. 114.

Per Øhrgaard

European – and to a certain extent to American – culture. Many German comments and essays from the first postwar years deal with European, not just German destiny. Behind this one may suspect the conscious or more often unconscious wish for relief and redemption: we all took part in the war, it is of minor importance on which side we fought. An anthology of poetry (1946) edited by Hans Werner Richter was called *Deine Söhne, Europa* – Your sons, Europe! but the subtitle ran: 'Poems by German prisoners of war'.

This is not all: There *was* no doubt a kind of common feeling of destruction: *Europa in Trümmern* – and not just "Germany in ruins" – was still in 1990 the title of an anthology of reports and features from Europe 1945-49 edited by Hans Magnus Enzensberger.[6] Hemingway's *For Whom the Bell Tolls* was widely read in postwar Germany. An American novel, but with a European subject, somehow the substitute for the great novel about the Second World War which had yet to be written. Anouilh's *Antigone* showed the consequence of morality (only recently reflected similarly in the film *Sophie Scholl*) that went well along with the philosophy of Jean-Paul Sartre (and with his play *Les Mouches*), and with Thornton Wilder you could feel confirmed that human beings are after all more or less the same in any province of the world. A kind of negative proof of these common feelings and notions was the fact that two major contemporary French books had been published in occupied Paris, i.e. under German censorship, in 1943: *L'Être et le néant* by Sartre and *L'Étranger* by Albert Camus.

So what came from abroad was eagerly received but also often seen as a confirmation and thus partly as a consolation too. Even more so the small volume by Vercors, *Le silence de la mer*, which told the story of a French family and a German occupation officer and made a sharp distinction between the officer, representing the idealistic and romantic Germany, and the Nazis, crushing all civilization – a distinction the Germans would also very much love to make.

Der Ruf existed from 1946 to 1948, a short period of time of which only the first part is of major interest, the months from August 1946 to March 1947. It was published by Alfred Andersch and Hans Werner Richter, who had been brought together by the Americans having taken both of them prisoners of war in 1944 in Italy and transferred them to camps in the United States. They took part in the U.S. re-

---

[6] *Europa in Trümmern. Augenzeugenberichte aus den Jahren 1944-48.* Hrsg. v. Hans Magnus Enzensberger, Frankfurt a.M. 1990.

education program, and they wrote for – but were not the editors of – the 'Journal for German Prisoners of War in the United States', already then called *Der Ruf*.[7] On his return to Germany Andersch went on with publishing, this time in his native city of Munich. He became the chief editor of the postwar *Ruf* – published under license of the U.S. Military Government by the Nymphenburger Verlagsbuchhandlung – and was joined by Richter from October 1946. *Der Ruf* took the subtitle 'Independent Journal of the Young Generation' (*Unabhängige Blätter der jungen Generation*). The word "young" might apply to Andersch, born 1914; Richter was born 1908.

This subtitle is important: On the one hand the magazine made the claim to speak for the young generation which meant: the generation that had been at war; from the beginning in the U.S. camp the magazine addressed itself to the soldiers, and this may also explain some of its later rhetoric. On the other hand the magazine claimed to be independent which did not only mean independent of political parties – they were anyway only about to be allowed and to establish themselves in Germany – but also independent of the occupying powers. In short, the editors understood themselves as the representatives of a young German generation that wanted to reconstruct Germany in accordance with their own – democratic – ideas and goals and not just by carrying out the will of the allied military governments. Eventually this attitude led to the dismissal of Andersch and Richter in Spring 1947 when the U.S. authorities got tired of their criticism that seemed to attract many readers: the circulation of *Der Ruf* temporarily reached 70.000 copies,[8] and it was no doubt read by many more (rumors that the Soviets had intervened in Munich to have the magazine shut down were never confirmed).

Already then, but especially later, when both editors had become important figures in West German intellectual life, *Der Ruf* was accused of being nationalist, and I shall give a few examples that may justify such criticism. But I also think that one has to take into account the fact that the editors and some of the contributors to the magazine had been through an American education to democracy and just for that reason felt justified to stand for democracy even against the occu-

---

[7] There were several camps spread all over the country, and Richter and Andersch were not in the same camp. *Der Ruf* was edited in the camp of Fort Kearney, Rhode Island (where Andersch was a prisoner), but had contributors from other camps as well.

[8] Some authors speak of an even higher number; 70,000 is the highest number counted in the magazine's colophon.

pants. Subjectively, although also paradoxically, Andersch and Richter saw themselves as a kind of emigrants: They too had now learned from the world's greatest democracy. In addition to that they had to bear in mind the target group of the magazine: Andersch and Richter were to persuade a large group of Germans that did not just turn from dictatorship to democracy overnight. They had to take the concerns of their fellow countrymen seriously if they were to avoid being regarded merely as an agency of the occupants – which happened to quite a few genuine emigrants.

Still, there is no reason to doubt that they meant what they wrote. And whether their contribution to the democratization of Germany or their contribution to a new German nationalism was greater is a matter of interpretation – as is the question whether you could have the one without at least some of the other! i.e. whether you can develop democracy without a kind of, say, pride. One should also not forget that nationalism – and certainly not always in connection with democracy – was still so widespread in postwar Germany, that one of the first moves of the Adenauer government from 1949 was to ask the formerly occupied countries for the release of German war criminals. I do not think that the chancellor himself cared much about those people, but his right-wing coalition partners did (in a survey from 1951 the West Germans were asked: When, in this century, did Germany do best? 45% answered: Before the First World War, 40%: The years 1933 to 1939).[9]

One of the most famous texts in *Der Ruf* was published already in its first issue: the essay 'Das junge Europa formt sein Gesicht' (The Young Europe Shapes its Face) by Alfred Andersch (August 15, 1946, p. 1-2).[10] Maybe it would not have become so famous if its author had not later made a rather spectacular career as a radio editor and a novelist. But then again, perhaps only a writer with this kind of future would have written that essay! It is a confession of a man of thirty-two who has spent years as a soldier in the German army witnessing Europe's self-destruction and who is now eager to participate in the building of a new Europe.

---

[9] *Jahrbuch der öffentlichen Meinung* 1956, S. 125f, quoted from *Vierteljahrshefte für Zeitgeschichte,* Juli 2005, S. 367.
[10] I rely on the copy of *Der Ruf* in the archive of the Akademie der Künste, Berlin (Hans Werner Richter's personal copy). Some of the more important articles from *Der Ruf* have been reprinted in later anthologies; but only the original provides us with the genuine context (including advertising).

What strikes the reader of today is the considerable naivety with which this German wants to join the other Europeans. In his own opinion he is responsible neither for Hitler nor for Hitler's war, and he writes as if all of it could be written off – let bygones be bygones. Europe is "a destroyed ants' hill" where young, unknown human beings are about to find and to play out their parts. They do not come out of seminars, but "out of action". First Andersch mentions French, Italian, and British intellectuals, also the Norwegian Nordahl Grieg and the Dane Kaj Munk appear in the list; he seems well informed of the history of resistance. This European youth is "socialist", Andersch writes, but at the same time "humanist" – which means that it will be to the left in social matters (sympathizing e.g. with the Labour government in Britain) but at the same time oppose any totalitarianism (read: Stalinism or just doctrinaire Marxism). The author makes reference to the existentialism of Jean-Paul Sartre, to the idea of identity of thought and action (contrary to the German *Bildungsbürgertum* that had either been seduced by the Nazis or proven too weak to fight for its otherwise noble ideals).

And here then come the young Germans:

From here [i.e. from the resistance movements] a thin, very problematic rope stretches across an abyss to another group of young Europeans. In the last years they too, without hesitation, invested their entire personality. We are speaking of the young Germany. It stood for a wrong cause (and not just wrong because it has now been defeated). But it stood. In exactly the existentialist meaning of Sartre and his fellows. In other words: The thin rope that connects the hostile camps is named: character [German: Haltung].

On both sides the experience is the same, Andersch claims – therefore the European youth can and will – or at least should – join forces in a common struggle for Europe's future.

It seems to us – despite all the crimes of a minority – that it is possible to build a bridge between the allied soldiers, the men of the European resistance, and the German soldiers of the front, between the political prisoners of the concentration camps and the former "Hitler-boys" (it's been a long time since they were that!) At any rate more possible than to build a bridge between the new tendencies in Europe, born by the war, and the thoughts of the older German generation, who out of tolerance did not commit

Per Øhrgaard

> *themselves, and who shrank from the final struggle [German: Einsatz] and thus gave way to the rise to power of evil.*

So much for the educated bourgeoisie, the *Bildungsbürgertum*, but so much also for the larger group of German emigrants, most of whom belonged to the same generation. (It should, however, be noticed that Andersch in a later article stresses the necessity of calling back the academic emigrants to German universities, and he also provides a list of names). To summarize the content of Andersch's essay: We, the young Germans, are not guilty of Hitler, so we feel free to participate in the reconstruction of Europe – especially if the Allies let us educate ourselves.

Andersch, in another article from October 1946, writes: "Out of the incredible favour of a complete defeat Germany possesses the strength for a complete transformation."[11] Andersch pursues this line of thought in later contributions, e.g. when in late 1946 he writes about the prospect of a divided Germany, made clear through the speech of the U.S. Secretary of State James Byrnes in Stuttgart in September 1946. If the Allies would allow Germany to stay one, Andersch writes, then the Germans would create a synthesis of ideas (socialist and democratic), "that might be an example for the whole world" (November 1, 1946, p. 3). So once again the world is supposed to recover by means of German virtues... Andersch – and he was not the only one – saw Germany as a kind of world laboratory: Germany had made experiments that turned out to be disastrous, but could for this very reason teach the rest of the world a lot. He apparently forgot that the rest of the world had not been keen on the German experiments and did not want to learn from the Germans.

Andersch finishes his article of November 1, 1946, with a phrase that could even be read as a threat: "The opinion of a 70-million people, living in the centre of Europe with a density of more than 200 individuals per square kilometer, squeezed together exactly at the borderline between West and East – the opinion of this people can, we believe, only be ignored by the world for a very short historical period." Here, Andersch – despite all rhetoric about Europe – clearly speaks as a German who wants a major role for Germany in Europe, and who also refuses to accept the loss of the German East. With this refusal, one has to keep in mind, Andersch by no means stood alone. His fellow editor Richter, further contributors to *Der Ruf*, but also many

---

[11] *Der Ruf*, October 15, 1946, p. 3: 'Die zwei Gesichter des Charles [sic!] Bidault'.

many others, all claimed that Germany would simply not be able to survive without its mostly agrarian Eastern provinces. Seen from the point of view of 1946 this is not just revisionism but a real concern: millions and millions of refugees were indeed "squeezed together" especially in West Germany that had always been the more densely populated part of the country. And as far as the number of Germans is concerned one can find the same argument in another article in *Der Ruf,* by the writer Walter Kolbenhoff: an open letter to the Norwegian writer Sigrid Undset who had expressed her hatred against the Germans. Kolbenhoff writes: "Still, we are sixty million living in the heart of Europe."[12]

Alfred Andersch – despite his call for the academic emigrants – sticks to his sharp distinction between the older and the younger generation of Germans. In an early article dealing with the Nuremberg trial (August 15, 1946, p. 2) he writes:

The amazing [erstaunlich] armed deeds [Waffentaten] of young Germans in this war and the "deeds" committed by somewhat older Germans, who are now on trial in Nuremberg, have nothing to do with each other. The fighters from Stalingrad, El Alamein and Cassino, who were in every way respected by their enemies, are innocent of the crimes of Dachau and Buchenwald.[13]

This is clearly the statement of a generation that feels betrayed by their "fathers", but in retrospect it is hard not to see also the wish for one's own exculpation. Similar views appear in an article from September 1, 1946, p. 1-2, by Hans Werner Richter, who was to become co-editor of *Der Ruf.* Its title: "Why does the young generation keep silent?" He may not be as aggressive as Andersch, but the points he makes are no different: There is a gap between the generations; the young people do not want to listen to the older generation which now wants to guide them. The old guys should have spoken up earlier; now their well-meant advice is of no use to a generation that has experienced the horrors of the front.

Now: did these young Germans really mean Europe when they said Europe? They most probably did, but one cannnot blame the Allies for finding nothing but nationalism in many of the articles in *Der Ruf.*

---

[12] *Der Ruf,* October 1, 1946, p. 13.
[13] This article is only signed "DR" = Die Redaktion (the editors). The anthology *Der Ruf. Eine deutsche Nachkriegszeitschrift* (ed. by Hans Schwab-Felisch, München 1962) identifies the author as Alfred Andersch.

German talk of or plans for "Europe" were looked upon with utter suspicion in the rest of Europe anyway. Especially during the last part of the war, as it was clear also to the German leadership that Germany would not be able to keep the whole of Europe under its rule, the Nazis had launched quite a few "European" proposals in order to gather at least the West European countries in a common defence against the "Asiatic barbarians". They also tried to gather writers in a "European Writers' Union" and set up a couple of conferences for that purpose. It cannot be said for certain if somebody like Andersch would have known much about this Nazi propaganda. What *can* be said, however, is that not many, if any, in the formerly occupied countries read *Der Ruf*. But the Allied authorities may well have had their doubts about a German claim to be "European" in the year 1946.

Later, in 1953, Thomas Mann coined his famous phrase that the Germans should strive not for a German Europe but for a European Germany. In January 2005, Lord Dahrendorf told the newspaper *Die Zeit* that he had always been skeptical towards this slogan because, as he put it: what is really the difference?[14] His suspicion might be justified by reading the articles by Alfred Andersch and others, but of course they deserve to be read in their context. Even so they may seem naive and shortsighted, but not as aggressive as they are now often interpreted by scholars. Anyway, *Der Ruf* shows that dealing with the past was not easy, not even for Germans who saw themselves as antifascists. It took much longer to get out of Hitler's shadow.

Hans Werner Richter in his articles also stresses the young Germans' wish for a European future. "They not only say Europe, they really mean it," he writes.[15] In an article from October 1, 1946, called "Germany as a Bridge between East and West" he realizes that a division of Germany may be imminent. "This however will mean the end of the German nation and the ruin of European life." (p. 2). He too, like Andersch, criticizes the fact that the German readiness to "go European" is not honored by the occupants, especially not by the French – who, it is true, for the first couple of years tried to prevent German unity and openly preferred the creation of smaller German states who would not be able to threaten France in the future. Another article by Richter, of January 1, 1947, bears the title: "Between Freedom and Quarantine", and here he does not hide his vexation over the policy of the Allies: "It is hard to demonstrate the advantages of de-

---

[14] *Die Zeit*, January 21, 2005.
[15] *Der Ruf*, January 1, 1947, p. 2.

mocratic life to a people being forced into a permanent penance" (p. 1). – Occupation forces are never loved, he states. It is true that one has to co-operate with them, but one should not expect the Germans to be happy with this situation, and the Germans still remember comments from the first months after the surrender, when they were accused of being all too servile. The *New York Times* then wrote: "At present Germany is a country where men have lost their dignity and women their honor." And now, Richter continues, when we try to behave with dignity and honor, we are accused of being nationalist (p. 1 f).

Then follows his attack on the French in particular:

They [i.e. the Germans] do not only say Europe, they really mean it. They do not just speak of peace, they live it. They turned their eyes in trust to France; in France they saw the exponent of a new European order. But what they now see is a narrow-hearted, petty-minded nationalism that cherishes itself by supporting German separatist groups in order to strengthen France's own security. (...) Sure, we are completely familiar with our own past. We know what has happened and we see its long-term consequences. We understand quite well the resentment and the aversion of the smaller peoples [!] against us (p. 2).

But nevertheless the politicians of Europe will have to broaden their horizon, to think about a European future. And then again comes the argument that the Germans are in a better position to see things clearly: "Maybe that we from our point of view, the point of view of a defeated, humiliated people, a people sentenced to penance, – maybe we see the dangers much more clearly and as being bigger than anyone else on this broken continent could perceive them" (p. 2).

To nearly all of the contributors of *Der Ruf*, France is the big obstacle: the fact that France opposes a unified Germany means that France also does not want a united Europe. Andersch in his turn writes about "The two Faces of Charles [= Georges] Bidault" who in his opinion was first a devoted European, and now (October 1946) has turned into a nationalist Frenchman. In March 1947, Heinz Friedrich, who later became successful and famous as a publisher (Deutscher Taschenbuch Verlag, dtv) harshly criticizes a reading of French resistance poetry in Frankfurt am Main: Well, the French have suffered, they have a right to be patriotic, "but what is the effect on us of this patriotism?" he asks, and he does not hesitate to answer: "We Germans, who after the catastrophe of 1945 finally want to escape from this narrow, destructive nationalism," – we Germans have to listen to French poems preaching hatred among the peoples... "The French hated the 'boches', they derailed their trains. Great! But in these trains sat for the most part Germans, who were, they too, just soldiers, because they had no choice, and who imagined serving their country no less than the French who caused their death."[16]

Alfred Andersch in his turn opens an article from December 1, 1946, with the following statement: "Even the most reluctant and severe domestic and foreign observers of the developments in Germany cannot ignore the fact that the German guilt account [Schuldkonto] is about to be balanced." (p. 1) This article was published shortly after the Nuremberg trial. And what should balance the account? The allied bombings of Germany and the expulsion of millions of Germans from Poland and Czechoslovakia. Nevertheless, Andersch has a point when he says that the notion of collective guilt or the perception of the Germans as forever unable to govern themselves probably will make it impossible to rebuild Europe. The world must trust the Germans – and in Andersch's opinion it can also do so: the Germans will find "the synthesis which the world needs"(p. 1).

An anonymous article of February 15, 1947, entitled "German Comments: Nation State, Borders, and International Law" goes even further.[17] After all, so the article claims, the average German who voted for Hitler is no more guilty than the average Englishman who voted for Chamberlain (p. 4), and one should better not forget "that it is by no means negligible what 70 million people in the heart of Europe think and to what they themselves have been educated by means of the hard language of facts" (p. 4). "Anyone who loves his native country should learn to love Europe. This implies that one has Europe's future in mind and makes a just peace with the Germans being the biggest population of Europe" (p. 4). Similarly and contemporarily Richter: "One cannot Balkanize and Europeanize Europe at the same time and by the same means."[18] There can be no European unity without a national unity as its basis, and national unity is inconceivable without a revision of the borders agreed upon in Yalta and Potsdam. Only the united German nation, according to Andersch[19] a little later,

---

[16] *Der Ruf*, March 1, 1947, p. 8.
[17] The "German Commentaries" used to be written by the editors.
[18] 'Churchill and European Unity', *Der Ruf*, March 1, 1947, p. 1.
[19] The article is signed DR = Die Redaktion (the editors); the above mentioned anthology identifies the author as Andersch.

"will create a people who like no one else in the world by its very own interest in survival will do everything to keep the peace."[20]

In hindsight all this seems dubious enough. But not only in hindsight. On December 15, 1946, and January 1, 1947, *Der Ruf* published an article by the English poet Stephen Spender who knew Germany very well – also before 1933 – and who at the end of the war was one of the experts on Germany used by the British authorities. Spender travelled in Germany and wrote about what he called 'the broken bridges across the Rhine'. Spender does not see a strong European movement of the time; he rather detects parochialism all over the continent. The peoples of Europe do not take any notice of each other, the Germans are still thinking only of themselves, disillusion and cynicism are widespread on both sides of the Rhine, and it seems at best unclear whether the present occupation will do more to bring about a European unity than the one after the First World War (i.e. the French occupation of the "left bank" of the Rhine). To many Germans it seems against nature that the French are an occupation power at all: in their opinion France should be counted among the defeated nations. Nevertheless, Spender continues, it is among the members of the French resistance that one first finds the people who understand that co-operation with Germany is a *sine qua non* for the recovery of Europe. And he then continues: "We ought to be very suspicious about anything reminiscent of a German youth movement, and this goes in a certain sense for any generation movement."[21]

Spender's warning is, of course, based on his earlier experience in Germany: National Socialism was very much a youth movement. "Youth must be commanded by youth" was one of its slogans, and Hitler was the youngest chancellor of the Reich ever. Spender even goes so far as to say that if the Germans do not change their mind soon, there will be a danger of a new fascism. It cannot be said for certain how much Stephen Spender did know of *Der Ruf*, but *Der Ruf* knew of him and printed his article although it must be regarded as strictly and strongly opposed to most of the ideas of the editors. In an editorial remark on the passage quoted above the editors remind Mr. Spender that his article is published precisely in the "journal of the young generation", which should prove their open-mindedness.

Once again: Seen from today it is easy to see the shortcomings of *Der Ruf*, easy to see that the European rhetoric often was a German

---

[20] Deutsche Kommentare: Jahrhundert der Furcht? *Der Ruf*, April 1, 1947, p. 3.
[21] *Der Ruf*, December 15, 1946, p. 7.

rhetoric. It is with *Der Ruf* as with the famous notion of the "zero hour", *die Stunde Null*. In his article of October 1, 1946, Hans Werner Richter wrote: "The young generation can begin from scratch, just where the development is pushing the others" (p. 2). But of course, there is never a zero hour in History, there was none in 1945 as little as, say, in 1989. In 1966, the scholar Urs Widmer in a famous dissertation on the "Group 47" showed that the writers of this association who wanted to write a new, purged language, had enormous difficulties getting rid of the language of the Nazis which had framed them during twelve years, for some their formative years.[22] Two decades later a major study by the Institute for Contemporary History in Munich bore the title: "From Stalingrad to Currency Reform" [i.e. of 1948],[23] thus pointing out that the German surrender in May 1945 was as much or even more a culmination than a beginning: the Germans – in the case of the study: the Bavarians – were neither blind nor deaf and had after Stalingrad figured out that they were not going to win the war. And as far as the postwar years were concerned, it was not clear until 1948 what would become of the defeated country. So 1943 to 1948 was seen as a continuum – which obviously is not the same as saying that 1945 meant nothing at all!

This is easy to see now. What should not be forgotten is that the Germans of 1945, and especially the young generation, subjectively experienced a "zero hour", and that they in a certain sense had to do so. The feeling that something new could be born out of the defeat was necessary for survival and for the efforts to rebuild the country – even if these efforts also aimed at restoring much of the former Germany (not meaning the Third Reich, but German tradition). Much was swept under the carpet even by people who thought of themselves as antifascist – see the remark by Andersch that the time has come to stop talking of the German "guilt account". In recent years even accusations against the Group 47 for being anti-Semitic have been raised; with little reason, I would say.[24] But once the question has been opened it is in fact surprising to learn how little attention is paid in the first post-war

---

[22] Urs Widmer, *1945 oder Die neue Sprache. Studien zur Prosa der 'Jungen Generation'*, Düsseldorf 1966.

[23] Martin Broszat (et al. eds.): *Von Stalingrad zur Währungsreform. Zur Sozialgeschichte des Umbruchs in Deutschland*, München 1990.

[24] See e.g. Klaus Briegleb, *Mißachtung und Tabu. Eine Streitschrift zur Frage: Wie antisemitisch war die Gruppe 47?*, Berlin 2003, partly also Ernestine Schlant, *The Language of Silence. West German Literature and the Holocaust*, New York/London 1999.

years to the extermination of the European Jews. Not that they are not mentioned! They are not missing when the victims of the war are listed; but they are so to speak just one group among others, not only in *Der Ruf* but in most publications, with the *Frankfurter Hefte* as perhaps the most significant exception. This was also true in the case of the Nuremberg Trials. The "singularity" of the murder of the Jews of Europe is a later notion – maybe simply because this crime seems still more incomprehensible the more remote the war itself has become.

Der Ruf no doubt took a rather radical stand and with its insistence on German self-education and self-recovery in some cases obviously got the "Beifall von der falschen Seite" – applause from the wrong corner. Still, if not at least some Germans had tried to keep a kind of self-confidence in the middle of the disaster, the rebuilding of Germany might well have taken much longer than it did. And even if it may seem almost obscene: If the Allies had not been met not only with servility, but also with a "national" German opposition, Germany might not have been able to develop into a country honestly committed to European co-operation and to surrendering sovereignty to the European Community. This also goes for the political rivalry between Konrad Adenauer and Kurt Schumacher. Schumacher once in a debate in the Bundestag blamed Adenauer for being "the chancellor of the Allies", in other words: a traitor to his own country. But the treaties of Rome were passed in the Bundestag with the votes also of the Social Democrats. They had opposed West German rearmament and membership of the NATO alliance because of its foreseeable negative effects on the prospects of a united Germany. But they welcomed a closer European co-operation – also a kind of "Wandel durch Annäherung", change through *rapprochement*, Egon Bahr's famous formula for the later West German "Ostpolitik".

CHAPTER 9

EUROPE AS A VISIONARY IDEA

The European Discourse in West Germany in the Decade after the Second World War[1]

Axel Schildt

The intellectual debates of the first postwar years in the western part of Germany were characterized by the enormous value placed upon the idea of Europe. In the aftermath of the bankruptcy of nationalistic hubris, this idea presented a comforting vision of a future political order. During the first postwar decades in the discourse around Europe, no steps were taken along this path at first, and then later just a few steps, and the upcoming concrete problems and conflicting interests of the European community were still unknown.

The lively West German discourse around Europe, seen especially in topical cultural and political magazines and in prominent book publications, did not represent a thematically new territory, but instead reflected a historical pattern of ideas which were a continuation of the interwar period.[2] This was no anomaly, as the self-understanding of the newly reconstituted bourgeois society during the reconstruction of

---

[1] This article is based on reflections in: Axel Schildt, 'Europa als visionäre Idee und gesellschaftliche Realität', in: Wilfried Loth (ed.), *Das europäische Projekt zu Beginn des 21. Jahrhunderts*, Opladen 2001, pp. 99-117; Axel Schildt, 'Der Europa-Gedanke in der westdeutschen Ideenlandschaft des ersten Nachkriegsjahrzehnts (1945-1955)', in: Michel Grunewald (ed.), *Le Discours Européen dans les Revues Allemandes (1945-1955)*, Bern 2001, pp. 15-30.

[2] This impression from the reading of different contemporary books and magazines has to be compared with the commentaries of important daylies and weeklies.

Axel Schildt

West Germany actually lived to a great extent within the conceptual framework which had been discussed during the Weimar Republic in particular.

It would be inaccurate to start from the assumption that hybridized Greater German nationalism was simply being transformed into a supranational European concept. In fact, during the interwar period, as well as in the "Third Reich", geopolitical conceptualizing, in which Europe would take a decisive role in world politics,[3] was never interrupted; instead, characteristically, it was radicalized, as it had been before and during the First World War. A frequently cited formula was *Raumverbundenheit* plus *Kulturgemeinschaft,* or "spatial ties" plus "cultural community" (August Winnig 1937).[4] A continental Europe under German leadership, in association with Eastern Europe as an economically complementary area: this vision of a "Europe under the swastika" appeared to be emerging as a permanent reality during the first half of the Second World War.[5] In order to adequately understand the trends of public discourse after the war, one must mention that in Nazi and especially in SS propaganda, European cultural diversity was repeatedly presented as a value worth protecting.[6] However, this European-occidental ideology also found resonance among Hitler's opponents, the nationalist-conservative *Frondeurs* of 20 July 1944,[7] which significantly helped to widen its appeal after the war.

---

[3] Especially well known – but not the only project of this kind – was the Paneuropa idea of earl Coudenhove-Kalergi; cf. Rolf Schneider, *Europas Einigung und das Problem Deutschland. Vorgeschichte und Anfänge*, Frankfurt/M. 1999; Oliver Burgard, *Das gemeinsame Europa – von der politischen Utopie zum außenpolitischen Programm*, Frankfurt/M. 1999; Wilfried Loth, *Der Weg nach Europa. Geschichte der europäischen Integration 1939-1957*, Göttingen 1990; Vanessa Conze, *Das Europa der Deutschen. Ideen von Europa in Deutschland zwischen Reichstradition und Westorientierung (1920-1970)*, Munich 2005; cf. for the literary field Paul Michael Lützeler (ed.), *Plädoyer für Europa. Stellungnahmen deutschsprachiger Schriftsteller 1915-1945*, Frankfurt/M. 1987; Paul Michael Lützeler, *Die Schriftsteller und Europa. Von der Romantik bis zur Gegenwart*, Baden-Baden 1998.

[4] August Winnig, *Europa. Gedanken eines Deutschen*, Berlin 1937, p. 9.

[5] Willi A. Boelcke, 'Die „europäische Wirtschaftspolitik" des Nationalsozialismus', in: *Historische Mitteilungen* 5, 1992, pp. 194-232.

[6] Cf. Werner Neulen, *Eurofaschismus und der Zweite Weltkrieg. Europas verratene Söhne*, Munich 1980; Jürgen Elvert, '„Germanen" und "Imperialisten". Zwei Europakonzepte aus nationalsozialistischer Zeit', in: *Historische Mitteilungen*, 5, 1992, pp. 161-184.

[7] Cf. die Dokumentation von Walter Lipgens (ed.), *Europa-Föderationspläne der Widerstandsbewegungen 1940-1945*, Munich 1968.

Considering the history of European thought up to and including the Third Reich, it would only at first glance seem surprising that the supranational European discourse after the Second World War, aside from a narrow counter-elite (including some returning exiles)[8] under the aegis of the Allied occupation powers, was largely being carried on by writers who had already for some time been covering this subject in Germany. Certainly they had to reorientate themselves within a new political framework. It was not especially difficult to see that Germany, after being occupied and split into four zones, would play no leading political role for some time. Unlike after the First World War, there was no dreaming about revenge or about preparing for a new war.[9] It was like the end of revolutions, like being thrown into a world dominated by modern global powers, be it in Soviet or American form. An elegiac mood dominated, and German state power was replaced by the European spirit, which functioned as a redeeming hope. It was symptomatic that intellectuals in defeated Germany seemed particularly affected by European ideas, and that even conservative-revolutionary figures of the Weimar era were now pointing in this direction, for example Hans Freyer in 1948 with his voluminous *World History of Europe*.[10] European propaganda even offered the possibility of presenting West Germans as model students of supranationalism who were faithful to Western Europe; in *Monat* magazine in 1954, economist Wilhelm Röpke criticized the supposed "anti-Germanism" of other Western countries as the biggest obstacle towards the "destiny of European integration".[11]

---

[8] Cf. Klaus Voigt, 'Europäische Föderation und neuer Völkerbund. Die Diskussion im deutschen Exil zur Gestaltung der internationalen Beziehungen nach dem Krieg', in: Thomas Koebner et al, (eds.), *Deutschland nach Hitler. Zukunftspläne im Exil und aus der Besatzungszeit 1939-1949*, Opladen 1987, pp. 104-122; Klaus Voigt (ed.), *Friedenssicherung und europäische Einigung. Ideen des deutschen Exils*, Frankfurt/M. 1988; Hinweise zur neueren Literatur in Claus-Dieter Krohn/Patrik von zur Mühlen (eds.), *Rückkehr und Aufbau nach 1945. Deutsche Remigranten im öffentlichen Leben Nachkriegsdeutschlands*, Marburg 1997; Boris Schilmar, *Der Europadiskurs im deutschen Exil 1933-1945*, Munich 2004.

[9] Cf. Gottfried Niedhart and Dieter Riesenberger (eds.), *Lernen aus dem Krieg? Deutsche Nachkriegszeiten 1918 und 1945: Beiträge zur historischen Friedensforschung*, Munich 1992.

[10] Hans Freyer, *Weltgeschichte Europas*, 2 Volumes, Wiesbaden 1948 (^{2}1954); cf. Axel Schildt, 'Deutschlands Platz in einem christlichen Abendland. Konservative Publizisten aus dem Tatkreis in der Kriegs- und Nachkriegszeit', in: Koebner et al, 1987, pp. 344-369.

[11] Wilhelm Röpke, 'Antigermanismus', in: *Der Monat* 6, 1954, Heft 65, pp. 534-538, here p. 535.

Axel Schildt

Europe as a Third Power – National Neutralism

The German defeat was at the same time a chance to invoke Europe as a "Third Power",[12] which was thought of in largely intellectual and spiritual categories, and only vaguely in governmental and intergovernmental ones. From the leftist Catholicism of the *Frankfurter Hefte* of Walter Dirks and Eugen Kogon to Protestant national-conservative circles in the German Evangelic Church, from Hans Werner's literary magazine *Ruf* and Social Democrat theoreticians such as Richard Löwenthal to neo-liberal writers such as Wilhelm Röpke and Christian Democrat party leaders such as Jakob Kaiser, the idea of a European Third Power was propagated in the early postwar years as a way of preventing a global confrontation between the two big Allied powers, which, after a strategic alliance necessitated by Hitler, were now obviously on a course towards confrontation.

These ideas set within the framework of Europe as a Third Power, itself a product of the interwar period,[13] became the nucleus of three ideological currents which can be differentiated by an admittedly idealized typology, and which took shape at the beginning of the Cold War and continued through it. The first of these currents can be understood as a self-conscious adherence to the idea of a politically independent Europe as a Third Power, despite developments in world politics which were pushing for a commitment towards thinking in Blocs, be it Eastern or Western. In this perspective, conceptions of a Third Power were increasingly combined with "nationalist-neutralist positions", which insisted on at least prioritizing the recovery of German unity before pursuing Western integration.

In oversimplistic terms, one could say that German nationalism after the Second World War was to be found primarily on the political left, which found itself in opposition, weakened by polarizing developments in international politics, rather than on the conservative right, which could not (and did not want to) afford it, following the disgrace and catastrophe of the delusional alliance with the Nazi movement. The uncontested leader of the West German Social Democrats, Kurt Schumacher, who famously called his rival Adenauer a "Chancellor of the Allies", would not let himself be outdone in his commitment to the nation. While the Social Democrats and the independent political left

---

[12] Wilfried Loth, 'Die Europa-Diskussion in den deutschen Besatzungszonen', in: Wilfried Loth (ed.), *Die Anfänge der europäischen Integration 1945-1950*, Bonn 1990, pp. 103-128.

[13] Cf. Gesine Schwan, 'Europa als Dritte Kraft', in: Peter Haungs (ed.), *Europäisierung Europas?*, Baden-Baden 1989, pp. 13-40.

did not shy from intermingling an emphasis on national interests with conceptions of Europe as a Third Power, the communists – completely isolated – constantly combined nationalist phrases with the vocabulary of class struggle. On the East German side, nationalistic propaganda was used to woo those on the extreme right who persisted in their "national-neutralist" positions.

Although the national-neutralist position was steadily losing supporters, the ideological conception of Europe as a Third Power remained very much alive in intellectual circles, at least at the beginning of the 1950s.[14] This even applies to the Euro-fascist variant of "Nation Europa" as a way to overcome the "war between brothers" through the creation of a "great family of white nations", as propagated by the British Nazi-sympathizer Sir Oswald Mosley,[15] a view which in retrospect was seen as simply an absurd maverick position. The same thoughts could also be found throughout pan-European propaganda[16] and in the columns of the elevated press of the early 1950s. At an anthropological-sociological conference in 1951, the prominent sociologist Leopold von Wiese called for a movement "away from the nationalism of the last hundred years towards a cosmopolitan cultural area" with the French, British, Italians and other Western Europeans.[17] An article in the *Merkur* welcomed the Schuman Plan as the "hope of humanity", and the author dreamed of "Eurafrica" as a "Fifth Empire", whose core would consist of France and Germany. "The goal of all progressive powers is the Fifth Empire. Only after this has been gradually achieved will Europe no longer invite the aggression of foreign empires through its provocative weaknesses as a Balkanized continent, but instead, prevent it."[18] It was no accident that the 1950s saw the last blossoming of the bizarre "Atlantropa" project, which envisioned draining the Mediterranean Sea to irrigate the Sahara, under European

---

[14] Cf. some hints in: Schneider 1999.
[15] Oswald Mosley, 'Zur „Nation Europa" (1951)', in: *Nation Europa. Monatsschrift im Dienst der europäischen Erneuerung* 19, 1969, No. 2, pp. 3-6.
[16] Richard Coudenhove-Kalergi, *Die europäische Nation*, Stuttgart 1953, p. 142; *Paneuropa-Friedensbewegung*. VI. Paneuropa-Kongreß Baden-Baden 1954, FrankfurtM./Berlin 1955; cf. Vanessa Conze, *Richard Coudenhove-Kalergi. Umstrittener Visionär Europas*, Göttingen 2004.
[17] Cit. Karl Gustav Specht, 'Zweite anthropologisch-soziologische Konferenz in Mainz', in: *Schmollers Jahrbuch für Gesetzgebung, Verwaltung und Volkswirtschaft*, Vol. 72, 1952, pp. 93-102, here p. 101.
[18] Felix Stössinger, 'Der Schuman-Plan', in: *Merkur* 5, 1951, pp. 409-428, here p. 428.

aegis.[19] The idea of a united Europe which could act as a great power upon the affairs of neighbouring continents was gradually overlaid with the new paradigm of Europe as a continent strengthened by its own internal market and technological advances, summed up in the phrase "Atomic Europe".[20]

The Discourse of the Christian *Abendland*

A specific – and in the first postwar decades hegemonic – expression of the European concept was conceived by groups dominated by Catholics and federalist conservatives, who did not need to appear in 1945 as formerly nationalist converts.[21] The "German catastrophe" (Friedrich Meinecke) forcefully illustrated that the Fall of God since the Renaissance, and secularization in all its forms (technological-rational thought, increasing mass conformity and civilizational advances), had led the entire Western world into a spiritual vacuum, and in the most extreme case into a nihilist totalitarian dictatorship (but it was almost by chance that it happened in Germany, and exemplarily so), and that all of Europe urgently needed to be turned back towards a Christian rebirth. Within the context of a historical-philosophical metaphysical discourse around the question of guilt, as seen in numerous political-cultural periodicals, a conservatism now marked by Christianity was able to renew its spiritual hegemony, and was finally successful in putting enlightenment and modernity in the dock. It is evident that this metaphysical fog, in which everybody seemed equally guilty, went far in accommodating certain ideological necessities – not least those of the functional elites of the "Third Reich".

It was under these auspices during the first postwar decade that the concept of a (Christian) *"Abendland"* ("evening country", or the Occident) became one of the most prevalent concepts in political-cultural discourse. It is striking that, especially in literary and journalistic publications, each and every piece of Western culture which could be inte-

---

[19] Cf. for this plan Alexander Gall. *Das Atlantropa-Projekt. Die Geschichte einer gescheiterten Vision. Hermann Sörgel und die Absenkung des Mittelmeeres*, Frankfurt/M./New York 1998.

[20] Cf. Franz Etzel, 'Atom-Europa von Morgen', in: *Politische Meinung* 2, 1957/II, Heft 16, pp. 203-227.

[21] Cf. for the following Axel Schildt, *Zwischen Abendland und Amerika. Studien zur westdeutschen Ideenlandschaft der 50er Jahre*, Munich 1999, pp. 21-58 ; cf. Guido Müller and Vanessa Plichta, 'Zwischen Rhein und Donau. Abendländisches Denken zwischen deutsch-französischen Verständigungsinitiativen und konservativ-katholischen Integrationsmodellen 1923-1957', in: *Journal of European Integration History* 5, 1999, No. 2, pp. 17-47.

grated into the dominant conservative *Abendland-* and *Lebensphilosophie*-based paradigm was seized upon, such as the thoughts of the Anglo-Catholic T. S. Eliot or the French poet Paul Valéry. Particularly high esteem was paid to the Spanish philosopher Ortega y Gasset, the much-read and bestselling philosopher of the 1950s in West Germany (where he was also well-known from the interwar period); Ortega y Gasset was especially forceful in defending an elitist individualism which was under threat in a totalitarian age. Ortega y Gasset never tired of emphasizing that "our intellectual wealth" does not come primarily from the various "fatherlands", but rather from the "common European storehouse".[22] High regard was given to precisely those European intellectuals who could contribute to supporting the dominant discourse in West Germany; this phenomenon is not surprising, when one considers general patterns of cultural transfer. It is also proven by the counterexample: there was a clearly vehement reaction against Anglo-Saxon and French cultural imports, such as the pragmatic ethic of responsibility of a John Dewey and the philosophical existentialism of a Jean-Paul Sartre; in any case, soon after the war and into the 1950s, Allied voices were already complaining that all the efforts towards re-educating the German bourgeoisie had backfired.

However, it became increasingly clear during the postwar years that a national "autonomous perspective of citizenship" had survived "only as a fiction".[23] German politics – and in the beginning, also German domestic politics – were still only possible within the framework of the two global power blocs, and were defined in relation to the fronts of the Cold War and thereby to the plans of integrating Western Europe economically, politically and militarily within a transatlantic alliance. Still, in the beginning there were only a few propagandists who openly assumed that in the long run the integration of the West would lead to the division of Germany; among them were Wilhelm Röpke, the neoliberal theorist who had emigrated to Switzerland. Already in spring 1945, he had argued for the creation of a West German state within the framework of a Western free trade bloc with a "complete separation of moral, political, social and economic principles" along the line of the

---

[22] Citation out of the article „Die Nation Europa" by Ortega y Gasset, reprinted in: *Nation Europa* 2, 1951, No. 2, pp. 3-9, here p. 7.

[23] Lutz Niethammer, 'War die bürgerliche Gesellschaft 1945 am Ende oder am Anfang', in: Lutz Niethammer, *Deutschland danach. Postfaschistische Gesellschaft und nationales Gedächtnis*, Bonn 1999, pp. 18-35, here p. 22.

Elbe.[24] But such thoughts were to be found only in federalist mouthpieces (and even there often indirectly) such as the *Rheinischer Merkur*, which, immediately after the war, had argued for shifting Germany's centre of gravity towards the countries at the cultural core of the West.[25] It was here that neoliberals and Catholic conservative ideologues could unite in mutual esteem.[26] In semiofficial political speeches and especially in Sunday sermons, which in the 1950s swore reunification, another argumentation dominated, namely the magnet theory (which Röpke had also formulated early on), according to which Western integration would become so attractive that it would isolate the Soviet Union and cause the Eastern Bloc to collapse. The Adenauer government famously expressed this view in the formula of a "policy of strength".[27]

The Western core of continental Europe as a political and cultural guarantor of "anti-Bolshevist" defence was (according to the undoubted consensus) the Paris-Bonn axis. The German-French agreement, as a general theme of West German foreign policy, also defined the broad current of political and economic press coverage. In this context, it should be noted that it was precisely the right-wing conservative *"Abendland"* ideology which, while objectively opening the door to the Western option, also served the bourgeois elites.[28] As Emil Franzel wrote in 1950 in the magazine *Neues Abendland*, it was Germany and France who should define the decisive motifs of the *"Abendland* symphony of nations".[29] Every continental European nation be-

---

[24] Cit. Loth, 'Die Europa-Diskussion in den deutschen Besatzungszonen', 1990, p. 111.
[25] Cf. the early critics of the construction of identity of „Abendland" and Europe by Walter Dirks, 'Die Christenheit und Europa', in: *Frankfurter Hefte*, 6, 1951, pp. 626-637, here p. 635.
[26] There was also a left liberal version of European federalist ideology in the first years after the Second World War; cf. Otto Lehmann-Russbueldt, *Europa den Europäern*, Hamburg 1948, pp. 90-91; *Der Kampf um den Frieden. Ein neuer Weltkrieg oder eine neue Ordnung? Führende Politiker und Wissenschaftler aus allen Ländern und allen Lagern fordern als Ausweg der Krisis der Gegenwart ein föderiertes Europa in einer föderierten Welt*, Koblenz 1948, p. 105.
[27] Cf. Wolfgang Bergsdorf, *Herrschaft und Sprache. Studien zur politischen Terminologie der Bundesrepublik Deutschland*, Pfullingen 1983; Edgar Wolfrum, *Geschichtspolitik in der Bundesrepublik Deutschland. Der Weg zur bundesrepublikanischen 1948-1990*, Darmstadt 1999.
[28] Heinz Hürten, 'Der Topos vom christlichen Abendland in Literatur und Publizistik nach den beiden Weltkriegen', in: Albrecht Langner (ed.), *Katholizismus, nationaler Gedanke und Europa seit 1800*, Paderborn 1985, pp. 131-154, here p. 154.
[29] Emil Franzel, 'Frankreich und Deutschland als Träger des Abendlandes', in: *Neues Abendland* 5, 1950, pp. 1-4, here p. 4

longed to this orchestra, including Spain and Portugal, which were pointedly and repeatedly mentioned. The glorification of right-wing dictatorial regimes on the Iberian peninsula as reliable pillars of *Abendland* thought sometimes took bizarre forms in the right-wing Catholic press of the 1950s.

Precisely these press efforts at including Franco and Salazar in the defence against Bolshevism showed that the struggle against the totalitarian "demon" was not to be fought under the banner of liberal freedom, but rather as a Christian campaign against the "Antichrist". Liberalism was seen as simply a milder variation on, or a precursor to, the threat of Bolshevism; at the very least, it undermined the spiritual resolve of Western defences.

In this regard, Catholic ideas regarding the Great Schism were also sometimes incorporated. In 1963, according to the Catholic magazine *Neue Ordnung*, it was still held as necessarily true that: "The Soviet Union is not part of this continent. Russia remains foreign to the intellectual and cultural life of Europe, it stands in opposition to the intellectual unity of the European countries, which are based upon Greek, Roman, and Germanic thought. The contrast between Byzantine Kiev and Latin Poland has not been dissolved by the enforced political conformity of Poland."[30] This shows clearly and unmistakeably that in the *Abendland* ideology of the Catholics the European border did not follow racial criteria, but rather religious and cultural traditions.

In view of this existential confrontation with the East, the unification of Europe (as frequently pointed out by authoritative Catholic *Abendland* protagonists) required the inclusion of England, which in the pan-European thought of the interwar period had still been seen as an almost insoluble problem, due to its overseas orientation. The mouthpiece of Jesuit theory, *Stimmen der Zeit*, illustrated this subject in 1960 with colourful language: "Things have changed since then: Great Britain has lost its world empire, and the *Abendland* is in danger of being crushed by Eurasia and ripped apart by the wolves and bears of the Russian steppes. It seems the time has come for England and its mainland neighbours to come together, to close ranks once again and renew old family ties, in order to withstand these difficult new chal-

---

[30] 'Europa. Raum – Bevölkerung – Erwerbsleben', in: *Neue Ordnung* 17, 1963, pp. 207-213, here p. 207; cf. for the alleged identity of east Roman church and bolshevism Gerhard Preuschen, *Europa – Probleme, Aufgaben, Chancen*, Wiesbaden 1962, p. 7.

lenges together."[31] At the same time, however, many intellectuals remained convinced that the British Isles were only provisionally part of the conceptual European *Abendland*.

In contrast to the mentioned currents in which Europe remained a Third Power, completely equidistant to the new American and Soviet global superpowers, the *Abendland* ideology left no doubt that a transatlantic defence alliance was an inevitable necessity, and that the military and economic strength of the USA was a security shield to be gratefully appreciated.[32] Pointedly, one could even say that for many *Abendland* ideologists, the intellectual bridging of the Atlantic was easier than that of the Channel. In the *Abendland* ideology, openly anti-American elements were pushed back to the fringes of traditional highbrow arrogance, and focus was placed upon the neohumanist analogy of Ancient Greece (for Europe) and the Roman Empire (for the USA); in addition, one was constantly reminded of America's roots in the *Abendland*.

The West – Liberal and Modern

The third current of the European discourse in Germany can only be seen in hindsight as a clearly independent stream. It was conveyed in the media by writers who, in the sharpness of their anticommunist arguments, at the same time did not want to be outdone by *Abendland* ideologues in the propaganda for Western European integration; among them, one sometimes also finds words and concepts that had been borrowed from the other camp, which hampers efforts at a precise differentiation as well as the already difficult classification of individual biographies. However, the crucial point is that this third current, with its option for an Atlantic alliance and a European integration, incorporated another image of the West which was largely free of the anti-modernism and anti-liberalism found in the *Abendland* ideology.

The conceptual-historical surprise of the 1950s was that as new, modernizing moments emerged ever more clearly during the reconstruction, the hegemony of conservative *Abendland* thought was not being destroyed by the traditional left wing, which remained within its national-neutralist limitations, but rather by those democratic and left-liberal intellectuals who had found themselves at first in a minority position after the war, almost as a counter-elite under the aegis of primar-

---

[31] G. Friedrich Klenk SJ, 'Der englische Mittelweg und das Schicksal Europas', in: *Stimmen der Zeit*, Vol. 168, 1960/61, pp. 173-185, here p. 173.
[32] Cf. J.G. de Beus, *Die Zukunft des Abendlandes*, Frankfurt/M. 1956 (USA: 1953), pp. 166-176.

ily the American occupational power. Among their ranks were quite a few exiles from Hitler's era, some of whom were now returning. As the result of a long-term research project by Anselm Doering-Manteuffel in Tübingen, we are now well-informed about the underground effects of this intellectual network's contributions towards the ideational westernization of political culture in West Germany.[33] In a narrower sense, it was the magazine *Der Monat* as well as the *Kongress für kulturelle Freiheit* (Congress for Cultural Freedom), whose international conferences provided a meeting place for prominent European intellectuals and politicians, who were drawn primarily from the fringes of Social Democracy and from left-liberal circles, and not infrequently also included disillusioned former Communists.[34]

In essence, it was not about presenting a uniform ideology in opposition to Bolshevism, as called for by conservative *Abendland* protagonists, but rather promoting a liberal and pluralist freedom of thought. The West would thereby become attractive by simply being more modern than the East.[35]

Conclusion

In this idealized differentiation between three currents in the discourse around Europe, it must be pointed out that despite all the distinctions in argumentation, there was always a shared bourgeois self-perception, in which the explicit or unspoken subject was a Europe of the elites.[36] While European integration was still restricted to political diplomacy, military alliance, and trade treaties in particular economic sectors, here existed the cultural goal of "building an intellectual common ground between the elites of European countries," as described in a study group report to the Council of Europe in 1957.[37] A comprehensive his-

---

[33] Cf. the instructive frame by Anselm Doering-Manteuffel, *Wie westlich sind die Deutschen. Amerikanisierung und Westernisierung im 20. Jahrhundert*, Göttingen 1999.
[34] Cf. Michael Hochgeschwender, *Freiheit in der Offensive? Der Kongreß für kulturelle Freiheit und die Deutschen*, Munich 1998.
[35] Cf. Axel Schildt, 'Ende der Ideologien? Politisch-ideologische Strömungen in den 50er Jahren', in: Axel Schildt and Arnold Sywottek (eds.), *Modernisierung im Wiederaufbau. Die westdeutsche Gesellschaft der 50er Jahre*, Bonn 1993 (aktualisierte Studienausgabe 1998), pp. 627-635.
[36] Cf. for example Martin Göhring (ed.), *Europa – Erbe und Aufgabe*. Internationaler Gelehrtenkongress, Mainz 1955, Wiesbaden 1956.
[37] Max Beloff, *Europa und die Europäer. Eine internationale Diskussion. Mit einer Einführung von Denis de Rougemont*, Köln 1959, p. 385; this is a report on the discussions of an international study group of the European Council 1953-1957; cf.

tory of the numerous permanent institutions created for this purpose (such as the Collège d'Europe in Brugge, the Europa-Kolleg in Hamburg, or the countless informal forums from the Ruhrfestspiele in Recklinghausen to the Aachener Karlspreis) which could put a conceptual-historical analysis on firmer ground, is, however, only just in the making. In any case, the increasing Europeanization of contemporary history is now calling for corresponding research interests.[38]

---

for the activities of this group Judith Kruse, *Europäische Kulturpolitik am Beispiel des Europarates*, Münster/Hamburg 1993, pp. 36-48.

[38] Cf. Henry Brugmans, 'Erziehung zum Europäer', in: *Frankfurter Hefte* 5, 1950, pp. 801-803 (Brugmans, a leading Dutch representative of the European federalists, was head of the Bruges Collège D'Europe); *Probleme der Einigung Europas (Europäische Wochen in Hamburg)*. Schriftenreihe zur europäischen Integration. Organ des Europa-Kollegs in Hamburg, Düsseldorf 1957; the Union of European Institutes (AIEE, founded 1951) had 19 members at the end of the 1950s, including seven in West Germany, two in Austria, four in France, two in Italy, two in Spain, and one in Belgium (Friedrich Schneider, *Europäische Erziehung. Die Europa-Idee und die theoretische und praktische Pädagogik*, Freiburg 1959, p. 30).

CONTRIBUTORS

Egon Bahr was born in 1922. After the war he worked as a journalist for many years. He joined the Social Democratic Party in 1956 and became head of the Press and Information Department at Willy Brandts office in West Berlin 1960-66, where he played a major role in evolving what was later to be known as the *Neue Ostpolitik* ("Change through *rapprochement*"). A chief negotiator at the Moscow and Warsaw Treaties in 1970, he had become Ministerialdirektor in the Foreign Ministry in 1966, and as Staatssekretär in Brandts *Bundeskanzleramt* 1969-72 he was one of Brandts closest collaborators. In 1972-74 he was Bundesbevollmächtigter für Berlin and Bundesminister für besondere Aufgaben, acting as Brandts special advisor in German and East European affairs. He was a member of the *Bundestag* 1972-90, Bundesminister für wirtschaftliche Zusammenarbeit in Helmut Schmidt's government 1974-76, and chairman of the Committee for Disarmament and Arms Control of the *Bundestag* 1980-90. Beside a wide range of other positions he was direktor of the *Institut für Friedensforschung* at the University of Hamburg 1984-94. Co-author of *Gemeinsame Sicherheit* (1986) and author of *Zum europäischen Frieden. Eine Antwort auf Gorbatschow* (1988), *Sicherheit für und vor Deutschland* (1990), *Zu meiner Zeit* (1996; memoirs), *Deutsche Interessen* (1998), and *Der deutsche Weg – selbstverständlich und normal* (2003; essay).

Bent Boel (1959), MA, Ph.D. in History, and Diplômé de l'Institut d'Etudes Politiques de Paris. Bent Boel is associate professor at the Department of History, International and Social Sciences, Aalborg University (Denmark). His publications deal with French contemporary history, the Cold War, European co-operation and transatlantic relations. They include: *The European Productivity Agency and Transatlantic Relations, 1953-1961*, Copenhagen: Museum Tusculanum Press 2003; 'La France, les Etats-Unis et la politique occidentale d'embargo, 1948-1954', *Revue d'histoire diplomatique*, vol. 1, 2001, pp. 33-58; '"Americanization": Uses and Misuses of a Concept', in Csaba Szaló (ed.), *On European Identity: Nationalism, Culture & History*, Brno, Masaryk University 1998, pp. 217-35.

Contributors

Patricia Clavin, historian, BA, Ph.D. (London), fellow and tutor in Modern History, Jesus College, Oxford. Patricia Clavin has published extensively on the history of international relations in the twentieth century, as well as European history more generally. Recent articles include "The League of Nations and Europe', in R. Gerwarth (ed.), *Twisted Paths Europe 1914-1945*, Oxford: Oxford University Press 2007; 'Transnationalism and the League of Nations: Understanding the Work of its Economic and Financial Organisation' (with Jens Wessels) and 'Defining Transnationalism' which both appeared in a special issue she edited of *Contemporary European History*, Vol 14,4 (Cambridge: Cambridge 2005). Her books include: *The Great Depression in Europe, 1929-1939*, London: Palgrave 2005, *Europe, from 1789 to the Present* (with Asa Briggs), London: Longman 2003, 2nd edition, and *The Failure of Economic Diplomacy, 1931-36* London: Palgrave 1996.

Morten Heiberg (1971), historian, Ph.D., specialist in Spanish and Italian contemporary history. Currently working as Senior Researcher of the PET-Commission which investigates the actions of the Danish Security Services during the Cold War. Publications include *Emperadores del Mediterráneo. Franco, Mussolini y la guerra civil española*, Barcelona: Critica 2003; (with Mogens Pelt): *Los negocios de la guerra. Armas nazis para la República española*, Barcelona: Crítica 2005; (with Manuel Ros Agudo): *La trama oculta de la guerra civil. Los servicios secretos de Franco, 1936-1945*, Barcelona: Crítica 2006; 'Franco, Mussolini and the Spanish Civil War: An Afterthought', *Totalitarian Regimes and Political Religions*, Vol. 3, No. 2 (Winter 2001), pp. 54-68; 'Nuove considerazioni sulla Guerra di Spagna: la storia segreta dell'intervento militare italiana', in Michele Abbate (red.): Pensiero ed azione totalitaria tra le due guerre mondiali. Atti del Seminario internazionale di Orte del 5 febbraio 2000, Centro Falisco di Studi Storici, Orte-Civita Castellana, 1, 2000, pp. 43-62.

Carsten Humlebæk (1966), MA in Spanish philology and Ph.D. in History, assistant professor at the Department of International Culture and Communication Studies, Copenhagen Business School. Carsten Humlebæk has worked with the changes of the discourse on the nation and memory politics in Spain after the death of Franco. Recent publications include articles in the journals *Iberoamericana*, *Historia del presente* and *Historia y política*, and chapters in Luis Martín-Estudillo and Roberto Ampuero (eds.): *Consent and Its Discontents: Post-Authoritarian Culture in Spain and Latin America's Southern Cone*,

Nashville: Vanderbilt University Press 2007 (forthcoming); Ángeles Egido León (ed.): *Memoria de la Segunda República*, Madrid: Biblioteca Nueva 2006; Klaus Ziemer and Jerzy W. Borejsza (eds.): *Totalitarian and Authoritarian Regimes in Europe*, New York/Oxford: Berghahn 2006; Max Paul Friedman and Padraic Kenney (eds.): *Partisan Histories*, New York/Basingstoke: Palgrave Macmillan 2005.

Joachim Lund (1967), MA and Ph.D. in History, associate professor at International Center for Business and Politics, Copenhagen Business School. Joachim Lund has published a number of books and articles on Danish and European political and economic history in the 20. century, including *Partier under pres – Demokratiet under besættelsen*, Copenhagen: Gyldendal 2003; 'Denmark and the "European New Order", 1940-1942', *Contemporary European History* 13, vol. 3, 2004, pp. 305-21; *Hitlers spisekammer – Danmark og den europæiske nyordning 1940-43*, Copenhagen: Gyldendal 2005, and *Working for the New Order. European Business under German Domination, 1939-1945*, Copenhagen: CBS Press 2006. Co-author of *Danmark besat – Krig og hverdag 1940-45*, Copenhagen: Høst & Søn 2005.

Axel Schildt (1951), historian, Dr.Habil., professor at University of Hamburg, director of Forschungsstelle für Zeitgeschichte. Axel Schildt has published numerous monographs and volumes on German and European social, cultural and intellectual history in the 20th century, including (recently): *Die Bundesrepublik der sechziger Jahre*, Bonn: Bundeszentrale für politische Bildung 2005; as editor (together with Detlef Siegfried): *Between Marx and Coca-Cola. Youth Cultures in Changing European Societies, 1960-1980*, New York/Oxford: Berghahn Books 2006; *Die Sozialgeschichte der Bundesrepublik Deutschland bis 1989/90*, München: Oldenbourg 2007.

Jørgen Sevaldsen (1942), historian, associate professor in the Department of English, Germanic and Romance Studies at the University of Copenhagen. His research interests lie in the fields of contemporary British history and modern Anglo-Danish relations. Among his recent publications are: *Britain and Denmark, Political, Economic and Cultural Relations in the 19th and 20th Centuries,* Copenhagen: Museum Tusculanum 2003 (ed.); *Churchill: Statsmand og Myte,* København: Aschehoug 2004, and *Montgomery: Danmarks Befrier,* København, Aschehoug 2007.

Contributors

Per Øhrgaard (1944), dr.phil., professor of German literature at the University of Copenhagen 1980-2007; visiting professor at Copenhagen Business School from 2003; full professor from 2007 (International Center for Business and Politics). Per Øhrgaard is the author of numerous books and articles on German literature, culture, and history, he has translated several works of German literature, and he often comments on German affairs in the Danish media. His books include *Die Genesung des Narcissus. Eine Studie zu Goethe, Wilhelm Meisters Lehrjahre* (1978), *Gæld og Arv. Tre essays om Tyskland* (1991), *Goethe. Et essay* (1999), *Günter Grass. Ein deutscher Schriftsteller wird besichtigt* (2005/2007).